Advance Praise for

Living Green

The key word in this title is "communities." It'
too long, and it's inspiring to read these acc

— Bill McKibben, author *Deep Economy*

This is the book I've been waiting for, and the book that
will become mandatory reading for anyone interested in understanding
or creating quality communities. Fosket and Mamo have examined best
practices and social mechanisms that most contribute to sustainable
communities. They have looked at diverse places and the people
who created and/or live there to gain an understanding about
what most affects the residents' well being and happiness.

— Robert Berkebile, Architect and participant in the creation
of USGBC, LEED and the concept of Living Buildings

Mastering the metrics of green living has never been more important —
costs cut, kilowatts saved, gallons of water conserved, tons of landfill waste
avoided, and so many more. Most of us are in intellectual agreement about
the importance of sustainability, but it is in these richly detailed stories
that we can find the inspiration to act, and it's not a moment too soon.

— S. Richard Fedrizzi, President, CEO and Founding Chairman,
U.S. Green Building Council

Mamo and Fosket describe elegant and accessible models for
living more sustainable lifestyles. This book hits on the fundamental,
yet revolutionary idea that the roots of social justice and living lighter
on the planet, and therefore achieving a sustainable future, lie in
how we build our housing, our towns, and our cities.

— Charles Durrett, AIA, NCARB, Principal Architect, McCamant
& Durrett Architects, author *Senior Cohousing*

Living
Green

communities that
sustain

Jennifer Fosket & Laura Mamo

NEW SOCIETY PUBLISHERS

Cataloging in Publication Data:

A catalog record for this publication is available from the National Library of Canada.

Cover design by Diane McIntosh.

Images: Landscape plan: iStock/Valdimir; Leaf drop: Shutterstock/Adam Gryko

Printed in Canada.

First printing April 2009.

Paperback ISBN: 978-0-86571-647-6

Inquiries regarding requests to reprint all or part of *Living Green* should be addressed to New Society Publishers at the address below.

To order directly from the publishers, please call toll-free (North America) 1-800-567-6772, or order online at www.newsociety.com

Any other inquiries can be directed by mail to:

New Society Publishers

P.O. Box 189, Gabriola Island, BC V0R 1X0, Canada

(250) 247-9737

New Society Publishers' mission is to publish books that contribute in fundamental ways to building an ecologically sustainable and just society, and to do so with the least possible impact on the environment, in a manner that models this vision. We are committed to doing this not just through education, but through action. This book is one step toward ending global deforestation and climate change. It is printed on Forest Stewardship Council-certified acid-free paper that is **100% post-consumer recycled** (100% old growth forest-free), processed chlorine free, and printed with vegetable-based, low-VOC inks, with covers produced using FSC-certified stock. Additionally, New Society purchases carbon offsets based on an annual audit, operating with a carbon-neutral footprint. For further information, or to browse our full list of books and purchase securely, visit our website at: www.newsociety.com

NEW SOCIETY PUBLISHERS
www.newsociety.com

Contents

Part 2: Social Justice and Sustainability

Part 3: Personal Choice — Living Green as Individuals

Acknowledgments

THE IDEA FOR THIS BOOK was hatched one fall evening in 2007 as we sat around a kitchen table in Montréal with our partners Helen Fitzsimmons and Kevin Hydes. Kevin and Helen were enthusiastic about the idea, and their support inspired us to risk writing outside our usual, wholly academic genre. We are grateful to them both for their unswerving support throughout the process of bringing this book to fruition, for the great conversations which led to some of its best ideas and for being our first readers. For reading and commenting on parts of the manuscript, we also thank Rima Shore, Kathleen Ferrara, Lois Arkin, Daniel Pearl, Ann Zabaldo, Rodney Elin, Melinda Jolley, Nina Berkson, Kevin Edelbrok and Daphne Ferguson. For believing in the project thanks to Chris Plant, Ingrid Witvoet and the entire staff at New Society Publishers and for ushering it through to completion with gentle hands and a critical eye, our sincere thanks to Betsy Nuse.

This book is a collaborative effort with the communities and residents who agreed to share their experiences and thoughts with us as we conducted our research. We thank all of the people who shared their stories. Many also shared their homes, their communities and allowed us into their remarkable lives. We are profoundly grateful for their hospitality and know that this book couldn't have been written without them. Special thanks to Danny Pearl for being our first interview and for providing insights throughout — we are pretty sure he is a sociologist in disguise. Thanks to the people who not only shared their own stories, but acted as ambassadors for our project and helped us move it to the next level. Ann Zabaldo has been unflagging in her support and an invaluable source of expertise on cohousing. Lois Arkin has similarly lent her passion, insights and expertise about sustainable communities at every stage. We'd also like to give a special thanks to a few others who truly brought the communities featured in this book to life for us: Daniel Simons, Rodney Elin, Daniel Barash, Nina Berkson, Kevin Edelbrock, Dana Smith, Alex Hill, Melinda Jolley, Joe Van Bellegham, Margaret Fabrizio, Bob Butler and Valerie LivingWater.

Professionally, we are grateful to the Departments of Sociology at McGill and the University of Maryland for supporting our work and to the National Science Foundation, in particular Steve Zehr for his comments and encouragement of early ideas that have been nurtured in this project. Laura extends thanks to the research team at Ashoka — Kelly Joyce, Kate Herrod, Sidney Brower and Ben Nathanson — for many discussions about the importance of green spaces in people's lives.

Many people accompanied us on our research trips to these communities as research assistants, photographers or supportive family and friends. We express our thanks to Donald Fosket for his companionship and beautiful photographs on the trip up to Oujé-Bougoumou, Lindsay Shaffer and Heather Marsh for their excellent research assistantship, Helen Fitzsimmons for joining us and taking photographs at our visits to EVC, TVC and Folsom/Dore, and to Eliza and Hazel for accompanying us to the Washington DC sites.

Finally, we'd like to extend our deepest gratitude to our family and friends, most especially our partners Kevin Hydes and Helen Fitzsimmons, who are our cheerleaders, our inspirations and the ones that enable us to strive toward sustainability in our everyday lives.

Living Green — an Introduction

ACROSS NORTH AMERICA — alone, in small groups and in large numbers — people are living in ways that are changing the world.[1] From Northern Québec to downtown Los Angeles, we have traveled to innovative sites where sustainability is integrated into everyday life. We met people who consciously and actively pursue environmental goals as a life's passion. They are building sustainable communities as architects, engineers, developers, contractors or simply as people committed to forging better ways to live their lives. We also met people for whom living green is an accident of address — who live in certified green buildings and find themselves integrating sustainable practices into their lives simply because of where they live.

Some argue that an enduring paradox of North American society is a steady rise in environmental awareness since the 1970s with little translation of this awareness into action.[2] People are concerned about global warming, resource use and general environmental degradation, yet these same people are not necessarily making personal changes or participating in social groups that do. As a society, we know and care more than ever before about environmental problems, but many of us are not acting on our concerns.

This book is about the exceptions — and their number is growing. The people we profile are translating ideas and beliefs about environmental problems into concrete practices; they are living and working to enhance environmental sustainability in its broadest sense. They are not afraid to face what Al Gore has termed the "inconvenient truth" of global warming. The people and places we describe figure in a much larger tapestry of committed people doing extraordinary things to make our world a cleaner, healthier and more just place. We add their stories to the many who are enhancing environmentalism, social justice, human rights and democracy; who are resisting the steady march of globalization and the extraction of natural resources, and who are seeking to document and root out the effects of environmental contaminants of all kinds on the internal environment of people's bodies and health. As Paul Hawken asserts, collectively these efforts represent "the largest social movement no one saw coming." Like Hawken, we tell stories that challenge the notion that people are not acting on their professed concerns about environmentalism. The stories we tell show people living their beliefs. Their beliefs are not uniform, however, and this is part of the story we wish to tell. Living green is not something that can be prescribed or bought. It is a varied practice that is both old and new, that includes high-tech innovations and long held traditions; it happens out of necessity and is driven by various motivations.

Yet, there is some enduring truth to the paradox: it is hard for many of us to live according to our highest ideals and principles. What gets in the way? We began our research for this book with an assumption that one steep obstacle is the way that our communities are built and organized. As a result, we set out to explore the ways that communities can hinder or help residents' efforts to protect their environment. We were inspired by Bill McKibben's ideas that as a society, we need to shift from expecting *more* to wanting *better* lives. We asked what drives and supports people to seek better not more in their daily lives? We wondered about people's residential lives, the choices made at home. We asked: in what ways do buildings, the sites on which they stand and the social organizations and institutions that comprise them affect residents' well-being and happiness? Is there a connection among buildings, communities and better lives for ourselves, the environment and each other now and into the future?

It turns out that people and their unique connections with their built environments are a major catalyst for social and environmental change. It is in the mundane, everyday work of organizing and living our lives that inspiration for, and the possibility of, being good environmental stewards emerge. As we visited places where people are endeavoring to live with greater sensitivity to the environment and human needs, we found that there are multiple mechanisms built into the environment — both the soft and hard infrastructures of communities — which enable them to do so. In the chapters that follow, we highlight these findings from each of the sites we visited and conclude the book with a chapter devoted to the lessons we learned.

The Relationship between People and their Built Environments

The complex relationship between people's behaviors and their built environments has given rise to many schools of thought and a wide spectrum of theories. On one extreme, architectural determinism holds that if an environment is designed and built right, desired behaviors such as increased productivity or increased community will result. At the other end, the built environment is seen as merely a stage upon which the drama of human interaction unfolds.

Our own school of thought conceptualizes the built environment as a technology that shapes, organizes and structures human activity — and in turn, as a material (a symbolically meaningful) thing shaped by human lives.[3] Built environments are actors in shaping human life — for good, bad and everything in between.

The built environment is generally understood as encompassing all buildings, spaces and products that are created or modified by people. It includes parks and roads, electric wires, underground pipelines, homes and office buildings among very many other things. It also includes social issues, such as the impact of air pollution or the distribution of resources, goods and services. For sociologist Tom Gieryn, built environments are places where buildings and people are in constant interplay affecting each other at all times. Built environments have material consequences for people's lives. A building's structure, form and materials shape how we move, where we go and make mobility easier or harder for bodies of different types and abilities. Buildings themselves are necessary to the development and modernization of countries, places and at a small scale, to aesthetics and use, for instance, of one's kitchen or bathroom. Buildings are also consequential for community — shaping how people can or cannot gather together, how much privacy people have, how isolated they may be. The less visible aspects of buildings — the glue, steel, nails, insulation and other materials that make up their substance, the systems that keep them warm and cool — are also consequential: they get under our skin, we breathe them in as particles in the air, we ingest them as dust. They shape how we feel in a space, our somatic experience of being.

For as long as humans have created shelters, buildings have carried symbolic value. From cave dwellings to condos, from pyramids to malls, buildings have been designed to evoke meaning. A building's shape, design, size, location, components and style influence the ways we make meaning, including the ways we think about ourselves in relation to our built environments. The history of religion shows us that people have always built sacred spaces as acts of faith and worship. In every era and place, people have built residential environments that include markings of class, caste or other symbolic ranking. Size, location and distinctive features of homes have indicated various characteristics (rank, occupation, social aspirations, aesthetic preferences) of the people who inhabit them. Frank Lloyd Wright understood this when he did away with basements and attics in his designs, seeing them as markers of social status. He preferred horizontal spaces which he believed were more democratic. Designers of modern skyscrapers understood that their buildings concretized the financial and political might of developed nations, projecting not only the capacity for steel production, but also the extent of power and progress. Viewed in this way the attack on New York City's Twin Towers in 2001 signaled an attack on US imperial and economic power; the attack on the Pentagon struck at the heart of US political and military dominance.

Meanings of Home

Residential built environments evoke particularly strong meanings. Home, however conceived, is the most intimate of built environments with which we interact. As French author Gaston Bachelard wrote: "If I were asked to name the chief benefits of the house, I should say: the house shelters daydreaming, the house protects the dreamer, the house allows one to dream in peace."[4] In *A Room of One's Own,* Virginia Woolf also associated individual space with the ability to dream, to think and to create. Like many other thinkers, these writers valued home as a protected space not only for the body but also for the imagination. The idea that home is a haven is also highlighted by those instances where it is not. In his book *No Safe Place* for example, sociologist Phil Brown wrote about the particular affront that occurs when one's neighborhood is infiltrated by toxic pollution because of the way pollution breaches the symbolic border between the world of industry and the shelter of home.

Comfort, safety, shelter, independence and belonging are all common meanings and cultural ideals attached to *home.* The historian Kenneth T. Jackson traces these ideas to the separation of public and private spheres that accompanied the Industrial Revolution and the rise of the city.[5] At that time, the ideal of a single-family home, where one could take refuge from the big bad world, grew in importance. Home was also, increasingly, seen as a feminized space where white, middle-class women would keep house while their husbands worked in the outside world. Advertisements began marketing household appliances and products to women, making the home something that could be accessorized and improved and instilling the notion that it was women's job to do so.

If keeping a good home became seen as women's work, being a true man became associated with home ownership. As Walt Whitman said, "a man is not a whole and complete man unless he owns a house and the ground it stands on."[6] Of course, in the late 1800s, a scant number of men (of whom almost all were white) had access to this requisite of full manhood, and equally few woman were privileged enough to inhabit the idealized domestic role. It wasn't until the mid-20th century that social programs in the US and Canada began to seriously offer home ownership to more of the population — though, of course, still not all. Nevertheless, the idea that owning a single family home was fundamental to being fully Canadian or American — and fully a citizen — had become entrenched in popular consciousness.

According to Jackson, "Throughout history, the treatment and arrangement of shelter have revealed more about a people than have any other products of the creative arts."[7] Jackson focused his analysis on suburbia, which is now home to more people in the US than urban and rural areas combined. He argued that the penchant for low-density, automobile-dependent communities says something about a group of people who crave independence, individual space and private ownership. To be sure, North America encompasses all kinds of residential patterns: farms, small towns, reservations, big cities and the many types of intentional communities and other alternatives featured in this book, and each may be able to tell us something about the values and beliefs of those who live there.

Since homes are so saturated with meaning, it is perhaps not surprising that they have emerged as focal points for activism and social movement organizing. Whether on a very local level as a town rallies around the preservation of a beloved landmark or on a larger scale as communities organize against the building of an incinerator in their neighborhood, people's lived, built environments often provide the impetus for, or context within which, they take organized actions. Materials used in buildings are now understood as toxic or clean and as sustainable or unable to be replenished, and the building practices we use may exacerbate or ameliorate inequalities. Certain communities — often poor and communities of color — bear the brunt of environmental degradation as a result of the types of built environments established there.[8] Improving built environments, then, is part of environmentalism and social justice. More generally, buildings shape human rights and contribute (positively or negatively) to human health and well-being.

The Green Building Movement

Although built environments have long been implicated in various facets of environmental and social movements, what is new in recent decades is the growth of a green building movement at local, national and global levels. It is a passionate movement seeking to change the way buildings are designed so that they might better address the needs of the future. The movement reflects current realities: in the United States, buildings are responsible for over 65% of energy consumption, over 30% of greenhouse emissions, 136 million tons of demolition waste and 12% of potable water use.[9] Many of these materials contribute to poor indoor air quality and jeopardize residents' health.[10] The burgeoning green building movement therefore seeks to find and incorporate building materials and design strategies that integrate healthy materials, increase clean air and are in harmony with sustainability principles.

For most of human history, construction practices have adhered to today's most basic green principles. Buildings have been small in size, well positioned to take advantage of sun and shade and located either close to the resources needed for daily living or the transportation needed to acquire them. These green practices persist in many parts of the non-industrialized world; they have also continued in a sprinkling of sustainable communities across North America and other industrialized areas. In the remarkable places we visited, communities are committed to localism and sustainable ways of life despite the pressures exerted by opposite trends. As a whole, however, North America has moved away from these principles. The US and Canada, once full of open space, is now defined by a built environment created around cars, freeways and the single family home. The success of the Toll Brothers in the US makes this clear as "living lightly on the land" can be replaced with 4,200- square-foot single-family housing for those who can afford it and are willing to commute long distances by car.

In response to this and other building trends, the professional green building movement came into its own with the formation of the United States Green Building Council (USGBC) in 1993. The USGBC was the brainchild of David Gottfried, Mike Italiano and Rick Fedrizzi. Gottfried was a successful developer who became concerned about the environmental impact of building practices and was increasingly convinced that there was a better way to build. Together with his friend, Mike Italiano (a lawyer with a specialty in environmental law), they began to explore how they could change things. Initially working with pre-existing groups to strengthen environmental standards on commercial buildings, they soon realized there weren't any existing groups that could do the job. In 1993 they met Rick Fedrizzi, an executive at the Carrier Corporation, and cast him in the role of the first executive of the newly conceived US Green Building Council. They decided that what was needed was an industry-led coalition of businesses, organizations and others within the building industry who were committed to thinking about things differently.[11]

From a few hundred members in the first years, the USGBC grew to close to 16,000 member-organizations. Industry-led and consensus-driven, the USGBC is made up of a diverse, even eclectic, set of organizations. One of their strengths in changing local practices is the existence of chapters around the country who are steeped in the concerns and issues of their locality and tackle change from the ground up. Another is their rating system for green buildings called Leadership in Energy and Environmental Design (LEED). According to green building expert Jerry Yudelson, "LEED was the first rating system in the United States to hold commercial projects up to scrutiny for the full range of their effects on energy and water use, municipal infrastructures, transportation energy use, resource conservation, land use, and indoor environmental air quality."[12] LEED provides four award levels (Certified, Silver, Gold and Platinum) based on the number of environmentally related points achieved by a new building project in the following areas: Sustainable Sites, Water Efficiency, Energy & Atmosphere, Materials & Resources, Indoor Environmental Quality and Innovation & Design Process. Since 2000, additional LEED rating systems have been developed for existing buildings (as opposed to new construction), retail, residential, health care, schools and neighborhood development. As these have been developed, increasing awareness of social issues has made its way into LEED. But defining and learning how to address the social in building practices has remained a challenge for this group largely consisting of architects, engineers, manufacturers, developers and other building professionals. We discuss this challenge in more depth throughout the book.

In 2003, the Canadian Green Building Council (CaGBC) was born. Kevin Hydes, a professional engineer who had long been active in the green building movement and was at that time a board member of the USGBC, Peter Busby an internationally renowned green architect and Joe Van Bellegham a unique green developer who had recently led the design and construction of the first LEED gold project on Canada's west coast joined forces with the Royal Architectural Institute of Canada (RAIC) to form the CaGBC. The RIAC incubated the Canadian Green Building Council by providing funding, staff support and infrastructure as Kevin, Peter and Joe built bridges with the USGBC as well as addressed issues unique to Canada. As Kevin said to us, "We needed a national voice to bring together the various groups that existed in Canada in order to bring about effective market transformation. At that point the USGBC was ten years old and had already proven that it was a success performer." And so they imported the model, but for a uniquely Canadian context: they adapted LEED for use in Canada and mirrored the establishment of local chapters across the country.

Alongside the efforts of the USGBC and CaGBC, other specific rating systems have been developed to work on small scale and residential projects or to address the particular needs of an area or region. Various organizations have implemented *principles* of green building design (e.g. Greenpoint, The Hanover Principle, One Planet Living's Ten Principles, Deep Ecology Principles). Today there are over 100 rating systems to measure green construction practices, many of which spring out of regional green building non-profit organizations and networks. For example, in California the Greenpoint rating system, a checklist for existing and new single family homes (a multifamily list is in development), emerged out of Build It Green, a professional non-profit membership organization. It was developed for the purposes of increasing green home standards and, similar to LEED, provides an objective, third-party verification system that allocates points for green building or energy conservation efforts including energy, indoor air quality, resources and water, as well as other green measures.[13]

As a result of all of these efforts, green building innovations have begun to saturate many spheres of what might be termed mainstream residential buildings. Green building innovations are now found in single family dwellings, New Urbanism, the rebuilding of towns and communities destroyed by natural disasters, and the redevelopment of neighborhoods long blighted by economic downturns. In addition, people are gradually integrating an ever-expanding offering of green products, materials and practices into their daily lives. From solar panels, to LED lightbulbs, to energy-star appliances to conserving water and electricity, people are interacting with their built environments in ways that explicitly address environmental concerns. The net effect is a groundswell of living green and green building practices.

Linking Communities and Built Environments

A key aspect of building green homes, one that is gaining in importance, is paying close and careful attention to the building site. Increasingly, the emphasis is on building green neighborhoods, not just green buildings. New Urbanism has been a force within urban planning and architecture to bring the components of a *village* — walkability, mixed-use, neighborliness — back into North American planning.[14] The group BioRegional has begun developing One Planet Communities within North America (they already have several in Europe — London's BedZed being the most famous) where ten guiding principles ensure the community adheres to strict ethical, social and environmental standards.[15] The green building movement itself has begun to follow internal leaders like Joe Van Bellegham in taking the community, rather than individual buildings, as the unit of analysis. The LEED rating system recently expanded to include a category for neighborhoods; its 2007 annual conference GreenBuild was titled "Communities." All of this recent interest is for good reason: creating sustainable communities is important to not only the environment, but to people's well-being and even survival.

Douglas Farr eloquently illuminated the connections between communities and human health and well-being in his book, *Sustainable Urbanism*.[16] He described the vast numbers of North Americans living in neighborhoods which encourage automobile dependence and discourage walking or spending any time outside. Housing has developed to reinforce sedentary life styles, spent mostly indoors and in isolation from one another. At the center of sustainable urbanism is an intention to reverse these trends: to, among other things, create, support or revitalize neighborhoods where the requirements for achieving a high quality life can all be met without ever getting into a car. When sustainable communities happen, they not only improve environmental conditions, but they get people exercising, experiencing nature and breathing clean air both indoors and out. As creatures of the planet, it shouldn't come as a surprise that what's good for the planet's health is also good for ours.

But there's another way that sustainable communities improve human health and well-being: they increase *social capital*. By getting people walking in their neighborhoods, by encouraging participation in local economies, people become more tightly woven into their communities. Social capital refers to the ways that we are connected to one another through trusting networks and is often thought of as the glue that holds communities together. The influential writer and urbanist Jane Jacobs was the first to bring the concept of social capital to bear upon on understanding of what makes a city safe and organized versus unsafe and disorganized. Cities that are designed to maximize informal contact among neighbors are better in almost every way.[17]

According to many social scientists, social capital is increasingly scarce. In 2000 Robert Putnam published *Bowling Alone* to much acclaim and attention. His book described the unraveling of civic involvement in the last three decades of the 20th century as tens of thousands of community groups dissolved, voter turnout diminished, charitable donations decreased and myriad other indicators revealed a United States of increasingly isolated individuals. Putnam documented the toll that this disintegration of social capital has taken on everything from health to crime to educational achievement. In our research, we found that social capital is an important element in living green; it operates as a mechanism to support long-term green living. Having social connections and meaningful bonds facilitates environmental sustainability at both an individual and a community level. As Putnam noted, "social capital allows citizens to resolve collective problems more easily."[18] We certainly found this to be the case for the collective problem of environmental degradation. On an individual level, I can more easily recycle, compost, not drive my car (or even not own one) and generally consume less if I have a network of neighbors, friends and like-minded comrades to help. In his book *Deep Economy,* Bill McKibben presented the convincing argument that hyper-individualism has taken its toll on planetary health. Acting on something as abstract as the environment is more difficult in a society which encourages us in every conceivable way to look out for Number

One. When we have strong social connections or social networks, we're more likely to think beyond our own personal needs to something larger. To see how we are connected to others and they to us is to understand that our actions impact others.

But, instead of encouraging connections, our communities and built environments have increasingly done the opposite. McKibben argued convincingly that the solution to the damage inflicted by hyper-individualism is a shift to economies that are more local in scale. By engaging in local economies, McKibben said, we are exploiting fewer resources and taking less of an environmental toll. But, perhaps even more importantly, this engagement "requires that [we] reorient [our] personal compass a little bit. Requires that [we] shed a little of [our] hyper-individualism and replace it with a certain amount of neighborliness."[19] And such engagements in neighborliness can begin a cycle that initiates and perpetuates the change it is seeking.

The hyper-individualism discussed by McKibben is part of the social, political and economic change that has taken place largely since World War II. Within the social sciences, a definition of the very term *community* is no longer taken for granted. Often used to describe and constitute a seemingly culturally distinct group, geographically bounded area or close-knit group such as a family or a town, a community is today understood as far more complex. People belong to multiple communities at any given moment; whether by self-acclamation, by socially assigned label or by engagement in social networks we move across borders by choice and necessity; we align ourselves politically with and against many engagements; we interact with, move away from and form bonds with a far larger network of virtual and real friends. Community presently is an evolving set of ideas and practices.

Dr. Vandana Shiva, world renowned environmental leader and recipient of the 1993 Alternative Peace Prize (The Right Livelihood Award), understands community in terms of citizenship; she illuminates the connections among knowledge, power, environmental and human equity. The increasing and cumulative ownership of the natural world — seeds, water, soil, oil and other resources — is the starting place for her ecological activism. "Environmental sustainability takes place when people have a stake and a share in the rewards of the conserved resource. If people have the ability to drink water from a well and look after that well, and will suffer the consequences of contamination, they will not contaminate that well. People who pollute a well or a river are the ones who don't have to drink from it."[20] The challenge is to make these connections more visible in our daily lives, to speak truth to power and to shed light on the many actions that are taking place to resist environmental and social degradation.

The relationship between sustainability and communities is interdependent. The survival of the planet is not just about plants, animals and natural resources but also about people and resources. As environments become degraded, animals and plants become endangered, but so too do the cultures, languages and societies interwoven into the physical landscapes. In this context, the vividness of human culture and society as part of the very fabric of planet Earth becomes clear.

Highlighting the Social in the Three Es of Sustainability

When we founded Social Green, a non-profit research and educational organization devoted to *social* sustainability, we wanted to underscore the ways that the social is already part of built environments. This book is one way to demonstrate the many ways people are already integrating social, economic and environmental sustainability into their daily residential lives. The sites described in this book showcase ways that sustainable developments repair and protect the Earth in all of its tangled complexity.[21] They bring together human experience — with its attendant cultures, symbolic systems and politics — with the natural world. Everything is connected and interdependent. Paul Hawken equates sustainability to an infinite game. We play finite games to win, he says, but we play infinite games to keep on playing. "Sustainability — ensuring the future of life on earth — is an infinite game, the endless expression of generosity on behalf of all." As an infinite game, sustainability necessarily involves any and all projects aimed at preserving life or promoting justice on planet Earth. Hawken goes on to say, "Any action that threatens sustainability can end the game, which is why groups dedicated to keeping the game going assiduously address any harmful policy, law, or endeavor."[22] In this way, Hawken declared the fundamental interconnectedness of all sustainability endeavors.

Social and environmental sustainability have long been linked. In North America, the connection between the natural world and the human community is a foundational principle of cultures in both the United States and Canada. From 19th-century indigenous communalism and religious communities to 20th-century bioregional, ecological and commune movements, people have been creating various ways to integrate and, at times, separate from the distancing effects of mainstream society.

Concepts like the triple bottom line (economic, environmental, and social sustainability) and the *Three Es* (economics, environment and equity) prompt us to stay focused on not just one but multiple axes by which injustices occur.[23] As Figure 1 illustrates, these three axes are already irrevocably combined. When building technologies or materials increase energy efficiency, for example, the economic result is lower utility bills and increased affordability for residents with the associated social result of being able to stay in one's home in the event of retirement, loss of a job or other financial hardship.

Like other writers on sustainable development, we draw distinctions among the economic, environmental and social, but we do so to point to their oneness. In the everyday real world, evidence of the tight links among them is abundant. And while we will demonstrate these links, as sociologists our goal is to document our observations and insights into the third circle — the social — by offering our findings and sociological lessons learned as we traveled through cities, neighborhoods and communities.

For this book, we traveled across the US and Canada: from the boreal forest to urban centers, from rural outposts to coastal cities and Pacific islands. In these places we conducted research at selected communes, cohouses and lands that resist classification, urban ecovillages, social housing developments, condominiums and single-family suburban homes.[24] We offer stories of these places: accounts of the

Fig. I.1: *The Three E's of Sustainability: Environmental Protection, Economic Development and Social Equity.*

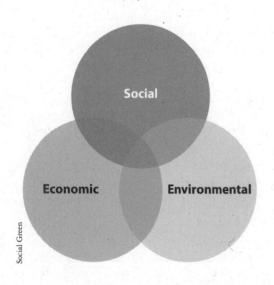

Social Green

extraordinary people who are getting them built and stories of the every-day practices of living in them. These emerged from our interviews with residents, observations of their daily residential social life and research into their development.[25] We tell these stories alongside photos of the people and communities we met and saw. Visuals are increasingly part of the telling of one's stories — from family photo albums to websites and blogs, people use pictures to communicate, organize and make sense of their lives. We do the same here.

What all of the sites we visited have in common is a vision of how it is possible to live differently on our planet. Each in its own way offers a beacon of hope in a world increasingly overrun by images of what is going wrong. We found a complex set of ideas underpinning people's decisions to live green: at times these are to be good stewards for the Earth and at other times it is to struggle against injustice and inequity. Often these motivations intertwine. Multiple paths lead to the common principle and practices of sustainability we witnessed. We believe that these practices can be incorporated into all of our lives, regardless of where and how we live. In so doing, each of us can help bring about many of the individual, social and environmental benefits that living green has to offer.

Part 1

Community

Back to the Land

DOWN A DIRT ROAD IN CENTRAL VIRGINIA, marked only by a small wooden sign with hand-painted lettering spelling out *Twin Oaks Community,* lies an approach to sustainable living that links land, community and social ideals. Informally, Twin Oaks is part of a network of over 500 intentional communities that exist across North America. Throughout time, intentional communities have flourished on this continent. Religious communes, cults, separatist communities and sanctuaries have all, at various times, been consequential elements of the North American landscape.

Fig. 1.1: *Twin Oaks Entrance*

For us, communes, especially those that emphasize going back-to-the-land as a great many of them do, provide an early and enduring example of living green. Whether religious or feminist in focus, communes tend to share key elements of sustainable living: they emphasize self-sufficiency, which means many people create local economies, grow their own food, work and live on site and generally maintain a low transportation and food carbon footprint.

19

Traditionally, intentional communities value communalism and a sharing of a variety of resources from appliances and cars to money and living spaces. This means that more people are able to get along with less stuff, and by extension, consume fewer natural resources per person. Within communes and other intentional communities, we see vivid examples of achieving the three Es of sustainability in practice.

For these reasons, we wanted to begin our journey of green communities at a commune; we chose Twin Oaks because it is a prime example of the back-to-the-land communes that emerged in the 1960s, but it is one that has adapted and endured over time. The ability to adapt, to remain flexible and change to meet the needs of current times, is another element of living green. Twin Oaks is also a community that has prioritized environmental sustainability from the beginning, and the varying ways they have done so can provide some important lessons for the rest of us.

Twin Oaks was founded in 1967 out of the social experimentation and political movements of the time. Since its beginning, Twin Oaks espoused a way of life based on values of cooperation, sharing, nonviolence, equality and ecology. Residents live by self-governance, collective responsibility, income sharing and an ethic of self-sufficiency. Today, "the campus" as it was described by our guide, Elsa, is based on cooperative living in tune with the earth and without the constraints of individual ownership. Twin Oaks is thriving and, in many ways, represents one aspect of what has evolved into today's green building movement: the initial desire to tread more gently on the earth by living in less energy-intensive, consumption-excessive ways.

Twin Oaks was modeled on the utopian vision of community in B.F. Skinner's book *Walden Two*, written in 1948. At that time, post-war prosperity, shadowed by haunting images of war as well as the great depression that preceded it, caused people to reconsider the way they lived. For Skinner, a pioneering experimental psychologist, this uneasiness provided an opportunity to radically revision social interaction and community. *Walden Two* was Skinner's only work of fiction, and drawing on his theory of behaviorism he imagined a utopia where children were raised communally, competition didn't exist, consumerism was discouraged and where egalitarianism dominated.

While *Walden Two* was well-received in 1948, its most fervent readers emerged 20 years later when 60s radicalism and counterculturalism meant much larger numbers of people were imagining alternative forms of living and of community. The 1960s and 1970s saw an explosion of intentional communities. Some emphasized an awareness of spiritual links between humans and the natural world, and a large number of religious communes were founded. Others were based in principles of localism or bioregionalism and emphasized a movement back to land and agricultural pursuits. Some were feminist, others feminist lesbian.[1]

Over 2,000 communes were said to have been established during the 1960s in North America. Many of these were short-lived, but others like Twin Oaks endured and evolved over the decades. Like other successful and long-lived intentional communities in North America, Twin Oaks understands and promotes a notion of community by intent and combines multiple goals and ideals that connect its residents.

Twin Oaks: An Experiment in Communal Living

Kat Kinkade was born in depression-era Seattle. After marriage, divorce, motherhood and a stint living in Mexico, she was living in Los Angeles in the 1960s, and was an avid folk dancer and member of the famed Los Angeles Troupe Aman. She read *Walden Two* and became convinced that it was a road map for a better way to live. In 1967, with six other like-minded souls, she founded Twin Oaks Community.

Within the original vision of Twin Oaks espoused by Kat Kinkade and her co-founders there was a merging of feminist politics with those of environmentalism and anti-establishmentarianism. Their vision and practice resonated with ecofeminism — a philosophy that understands the oppression of women and nature to be inherently linked, with the violence inflicted on women and nature resulting from male domination. Similar to other ecological movements, ecofeminism emphasizes unity with nature, but it also signals cooperation and egalitarianism, spiritualism and political action.[2]

While Twin Oaks is not an example of any single idealism, it represents a community built on multiple ideals that in practice are worked out among the set of current members living on the land. Twin Oaks

Mary Ellen Kustin

Fig. 1.2: *Farming at Twin Oaks.*

continues to function as an experiment in feminist politics. It is part of the Feminist EcoVillage Project, a coalition of intentional communities which holds feminist values at their core, and it continues to host a women's retreat annually on the land. Twin Oaks describes itself as working to create a feminist culture that doesn't limit or prejudge what a person might wear or do based on preconceived gender stereotypes. On their website, they assert, "Our commitment to fostering a supportive and joyful environment for all people — women, men, lesbians, gays and children — is an integral part of Twin Oaks Community."[3] At Twin Oaks, egalitarianism is a driving ethic and one of four basic values upon which Twin Oaks was founded. The others are cooperation, income sharing and nonviolence. These are not just abstract ideals but concrete practices to which each person agrees in order to join the Twin Oaks Community. As we learned more about the community, we also discovered that these four basic values speak eloquently to economic, environmental and social sustainability.

It was on a warm afternoon in Spring 2008 that we traveled to Twin Oaks. We arrived a little after two o'clock and were greeted by Elsa, a 33-year-old mother of a 4-year-old son and one of the longest-term residents presently living at Twin Oaks. She and her son's father resided at a neighboring community, Acorn, until their recent separation when Elsa returned to Twin Oaks.

Twin Oaks is currently made up of 85 adults on 465 acres of land with 7 residence buildings, 30 cows, 3 major businesses and 18 vehicles.[4] Much of the acreage is devoted to open space, and sprawling oak trees, dense woods, rolling green hills and meadows, wild-flower bordered ponds and the occasional barn render the scenery a picture of rural beauty. Walkways and roads are comprised of dirt and gravel. It's not all open

Fig. 1.3: *Greenhouse at Twin Oaks.*

space, however, and it doesn't take us long to appreciate how much of this land is providing sustenance to the community. The meadows are pastures for cattle that are raised for food. Gardens are scattered throughout, each taking advantage of particular conditions for growing and providing food for the community.

Twin Oaks residents live collectively in houses with about 10-20 people each. Each building is unique, built in sequence as need arose and money and time allowed.

The interior of most residential buildings includes open beams and a

Fig. 1.4: *Residential Building at Twin Oaks.*

wood-burning fireplace. Each member gets one small private room (many have loft beds built in) and members share kitchens, bathrooms and living rooms. Couples and individuals or couples with children can choose to share a room and use the other one for a living room. Refrigerators are stocked with community grown and produced food, and residents are also able to keep their own privately purchased food. For the most part, residents share meals in the large dining hall in building ZK.

A food team is in place each week to coordinate meal preparation and make decisions about purchases to supplement what is produced by the community. Although breakfast is not served (there is brunch on the weekends), lunch and dinner are. People can eat together or separately. The dinner meal draws approximately 50 people — which is the largest gathering of community members. Outside of dinners, the largest community gatherings at Twin Oaks in Spring 2008 were the weekly Ultimate Frisbee matches which drew players from within the community, from sister communities in the area and from former members living in Virginia.

Unlike some other intentional communities, at Twin Oaks there are no meetings that draw every community member because it is deemed impossible to schedule a meeting around personal work and social agendas. Interestingly, Elsa described the community as being very bureaucratic with many inscribed rules to the point that even a protest has a process.

Fig. 1.5: *Communication System at Twin Oaks.*

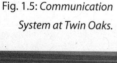

Mary Ellen Kustin

Yet communication seemed quite active at Twin Oaks. Each member has a work/social calendar (even children have their own calendars), and in ZK there are *Labor Finders*, duplicate calendars for everyone. Everyone has a job at Twin Oaks — working in one of the on-site businesses, maintaining the land or providing for other members' needs. Jobs are assigned based on preference or on what needs to get done. At times, there are sessions designed to encourage people to participate, such as playing music in the work area or having work parties.

Every work/social sheet is public knowledge in case another member of the community needs to locate someone. Communication is also facilitated through personal note boxes and message boards where individuals write and post messages on 3x5 cards — from messages of thanks to requests for carpooling. The Opinion and Information board operates as a response board to team needs and ongoing points of discussion. Residents can write and submit their own issue notices. The Opinion and Information notes stay up for ten days at which point feedback left on the postings is gathered and reviewed.

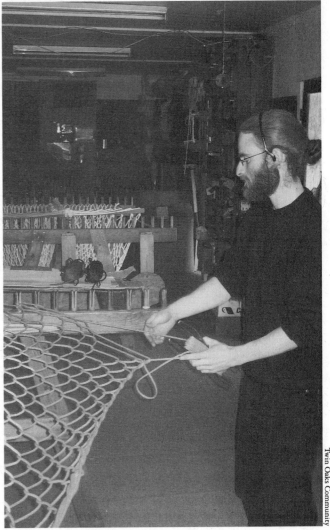

Fig. 1.6: *Hammock Worker at Twin Oaks.*

Twin Oaks Community

Living Green at Twin Oaks

There are multiple ways Twin Oaks enables its residents to live green. First, since its inception in 1967, community members have adhered to principles of self-sufficiency and living lightly on the land. Residents grow, harvest and produce their own food. Vegetables are harvested in the community garden, and cattle are raised and slaughtered on site for beef consumption. Wood is harvested from the Twin Oaks property by their forestry management crew charged with preserving the land's natural forested ecosystem and monitoring the land for dead and downed trees.

These founding principles have been joined by more high-tech green innovations. Today, if you visit Twin Oaks you will see several solar panels assisting with hot water heating and electrical production; you will find four composting toilets near well-traveled work and residential areas and there is a relatively new residential building that is technically off-the-grid. The community utilizes passive solar heating, thermal mass, superinsulation, thermal curtains and shutters, maximum natural lighting, cellulose (recycled) insulation, natural wood siding and high performance windows.

Twin Oaks also promotes green living through the establishment and maintenance of local economies. Twin Oaks operates and collectively runs three major businesses including hammock making (since 1971), tofu making and book indexing. Within this model, no one needs to commute: work, home life and leisure are intertwined and on-site, a factor which drastically reduces the community's carbon footprint. Of course, the businesses also contribute to the economic sustainability of the community. The income generated from these businesses allows the community to be self-sustaining and contributes to community members' allowances. Further, the businesses themselves are run with environmental sustainability in mind since the efficient use of resources contributes to the businesses' overall profitability, which, in turn, makes the community more self-sufficient and secure.

Perhaps the most significant way Twin Oak community members practice economic, social and environmental sustainability is through the strong value of sharing resources. As one resident described it, "By pooling and sharing resources we are able to reduce our expenses and the subsequent impact on the Earth." Money, cars, personal items, services and work are shared equally among community members. Residents of Twin Oaks come to the community surrendering most ties to income, assets and property and agreeing to an income-sharing model of living. Twin Oaks does not take over residents' assets or debts; yet to maintain equality they require that individuals freeze their outside assets. In exchange for community work, each resident is provided an allowance of $76 a month. Since assets are frozen and individuals subsist on their allowances and community resources, equality and social cohesion are created.

Through these practices of living communally, residents at Twin Oaks manage to equalize economic disparities: each member has, or doesn't have the same as everyone else. Inequalities along economic lines are dissolved. In terms of living green, this equalization also makes for a far less consumer-driven culture than exists in mainstream society. Clothes and other personal items are shared at a local swap shop where residents can drop off unwanted items and pick up new ones. Without private ownership, having things is not a high priority at Twin Oaks. Less consumerism means less waste. Here, people live with what they need rather than excessively. It also means less energy-intensive lifestyles. Because people are sharing, it means every single person or household isn't running items like a television, washing machine, dishwasher, computer and printer.

The way sharing cuts down on this community's carbon footprint is also evident in the way cars are shared, or more accurately, individual cars are rarely used at all. Residents are required to leave privately owned cars behind or to donate them to the community when they become residents. While residents can rent community cars at $0.25 per mile, most residents we spoke to travel by community van when they want to go into one of the nearby towns for shopping, health care or to spend a day off. Elsa explained that since residents have to pay to use an individual car, many residents opt for the more environmentally friendly and community-building option of the group outing. Group trips are run to Louisa — the closest town to the Twin Oaks community — once per day, to Charlottesville three times a week and to Richmond, Virginia once a week. Twin Oaks has cultivated a close connection with Louisa through these daily trips: Twin Oaks contributes financially to this small Virginia town by doing things like their banking there, and Louisa supports Twin Oaks by giving them access to aspects of life they can't necessarily provide for themselves.

The social sustainability of the community is also bolstered by a socialized health care system

Fig. 1.7: *Swap Shop at Twin Oaks.*

Mary Ellen Kustin

in which the community provides all basic health care to its residents. Residents are able to receive the care that they need including mental health services, birth control and preventative care. The Health Team makes decisions about the community's coverage and allows residents to pursue both Western medical treatments as well as alternative healing modalities such as acupuncture and chiropractic care. The community also pays for members to see counselors/therapists.

Twin Oaks is unique among the communities featured in this book because it has been around for decades and was originally built on low-tech sustainable practices. Yet, it has been flexible, adapting to changing times and membership demographics. In a 1995 article about Twin Oaks, Kat Kinkade wrote

> A viable community adapts to the needs and desires of its members much more than it conforms to abstract ideals ... There will be some determined core idealism, but otherwise compromises will prevail.[5]

Kat herself was a tribute to the flexibility and changing demands of community and also to the enduring social support that a strong community can offer. At the age of 70, Kat decided she wanted to try living in a house of her own, something she had never had the opportunity to do. She moved into a tiny little house in Mineral (near Twin Oaks and Acorn) and enjoyed planting many beautiful flowers, rescuing five cats of her own and bottle-feeding the occasional litter as a foster mom. When her health failed, she returned to Twin Oaks where she was taken care of until she died on July 3, 2008 of complications related to bone cancer. She was buried in the cemetery at Twin Oaks.

Flexibility and adaptation are themselves central aspects of not only living green at any given time, but in ensuring that doing so can be maintained over time. When Twin Oaks began, it was responding to different kinds of pressures than exist today. Such flexibility is also apparent as Twin Oaks incorporates technological innovations such as solar panels into their building practices. What it means to live green will not be the same in another 20 years as it is today, and successful green communities will, like Twin Oaks, be able to adapt to, and welcome, whatever kinds of challenges and opportunities may exist in the future.

Oujé-Bougoumou

An entirely different back-to-the-land story is unfolding in Northern Québec. In the James Bay territory along the shores of Lake Opemiska, the village of Oujé-Bougoumou stands as a hybrid of traditional modes of living and architectural forms and green technologies. Like Twin Oaks, Oujé-Bougoumou is the manifestation of people's desire to live in closer harmony with the land and with each other. However, Oujé-Bougoumou

Donald Fosket

Fig. 1.8:

Entrance to Oujé-Bougoumou.

is not a commune or intentional community in the common sense of that phrase; it is the reclaimed homeland of the Oujé-Bougoumou Eenou or Cree. For over 5,000 years the Oujé-Bougoumou Crees have lived in Northern Québec. Their history resonates with that of many Aboriginal, Inuit, First-Nations and Native American peoples across North America: discrimination, abuse, dispossession and neglect at the hands of governments and industries like mining and forestry have ravaged many communities. The tight connections between environmental and social justice are nowhere more stark than in the stories of generations of Indigenous peoples around the globe. Land is pilfered for profit, and communities, families and individuals plunge into poverty.

Québec has the largest provincial area of forested land in Canada — an area larger than the state of Texas. The land also contains rich mineral deposits. As a result, mining and lumber have been big business in this part of Québec; businesses have devastated the land as well as the people who first called this land home. Oujé-Bougoumou elders can still remember when some of the earliest mining prospectors entered their territory looking for gold and copper. Demand for these profitable minerals intensified, and before long mining camps, settlements and towns were established on Cree land. Villages were bulldozed. In a 50-year period, the Oujé-Bougoumou People were forced to relocate seven different times — their homes destroyed, communities scattered and connections severed. As the land was depleted in order to extract profit, animal populations declined and, with them, the means of survival for the Oujé-Bougoumou People who remained. Living conditions were dire.

In response to what was happening to their land and community and in the absence of government intervention, the Oujé-Bougoumou Cree staged a major political intervention in the summer of 1989. Declaring jurisdiction over their territory, they blockaded the access road to what was then their village, established their own court and convicted the provincial and federal governments of breaching their fiduciary obligation to Oujé-Bougoumou. This resulted in governmental attention, and by September 1989 an agreement was reached with the Québec provincial government, one which had been in the works since the mid-1980s. Québec agreed to contribute financially toward the construction of a new,

Fig. 1.9:
*Oujé-Bougoumou
Cree Headquarters.*

permanent village while also acknowledging a degree of local jurisdiction over a portion of the Oujé-Bougoumou Cree traditional territory. In
1992 the Oujé-Bougoumou/Canada Agreement was signed by the Oujé-
Bougoumou People and the Canadian federal government. This agreement
secured financial backing for the building of a new permanent village.
Thus began the green village that stands today.

Located in the boreal forest of the James Bay Territory between the
49th and 50th parallels, 45 minutes from Chibougamau and a 25-minute
drive from the nearest airport, Oujé-Bougoumou village is home to about
650 people. Street signs are in Cree syllabics, English and French. In
planning the village, three major objectives were defined: the village had
to be constructed in harmony with nature and with the traditional Cree
philosophy of conservation; it had to provide for the long-term financial
needs of its people and it had to reflect Cree culture in its physical appear-
ance and in its functions.

Arriving at Oujé-Bougoumou on a brilliant summer's day, adherence
to these goals stands out. The village is built in circular patterns, with
many buildings themselves octagonal or hexagonal. Most share a deep

brown color, and they don't disrupt the lines of the hills and forests of spruce and birch trees. At the center of the circle on top of a small hill, is the *shaptuwan* (traditional meeting place for feasts), and the two inner rings are lined with community buildings, reflecting the culture of sharing. Here is the concentrated center of residences and public buildings: Cree government offices, post office, bank, youth center, church, gas station and *dépaneur*. There is an impressive sports complex with a pool, ice rink and fitness center, a school, daycare and multiple playgrounds. A lodge sits on the edge of the village, catering to tourists for overnight stays and including a restaurant that caters to the whole village.

Internationally renowned aboriginal Canadian architect Douglas Cardinal was hired to design the major public institutions in the new village.[6] He worked in close consultation with community members whose input was gathered at every stage. The buildings were designed to reflect the structure of the *astchiiugamikw*, a dwelling constructed of a teepee-like wooden frame with its ceiling reaching the earth and covered with a combination of moss and sand. Some of the buildings are constructed traditionally, and others are stylistically akin but more modern. All of

Fig. 1.10:
*Shaptuwan Building
at Oujé-Bougoumou.*

Donald Fosket

the interiors are bathed in natural light from large windows and sky-lights. The doors of the homes face east, where the sun rises, as the elders demanded.

The roads are paved and sidewalks snake around the village, but large areas of green space (alder thickets, blueberry bushes and small willow trees) fill in the spaces between buildings and houses, often with beige sandy patches signifying commonly trodden paths between neighbors. Bright orange fireweed provides a shock of color to this landscape. Most of the land is left wild. A huge, magnificent lake hugs one end of the village, and the boreal forest edges the rest. Paths wend their way through. Walking around the property, the predominant feeling is of a natural landscape; the village is like a seamless extension.

Living Green at Oujé-Bougoumou

In this boreal forest of Northern Québec winter can last for a better part of a year, and temperatures regularly plunge into the minus double-digits. Providing warmth in this climate is no easy matter. At Oujé-Bougoumou a combination of traditional architectures and cutting edge technologies are used to produce energy for the village. The buildings were designed to take advantage of sun and warmth and are insulated to keep it in.

Donald Fosker

Fig. 1.11:
*Oujé-Bougoumou
Village.*

Added to the passive heating, a biomass generator brings heat to the village. This energy system takes the waste sawdust from sawmills operating in the region and converts it into energy to provide heat and hot water for the entire village.

The community chose to invest in a biomass generator after recognizing the potential that existed in piles of sawdust waste from local sawmills that previously did nothing but spoil the natural beauty of the land. A long and thorough process of weighing the benefits and risks of such an endeavor was undertaken by the community in consultation with various professionals with appropriate expertise. Ultimately, the biomass generator was chosen. It is a poignant testament to the interconnected goals of environmental and social sustainability that something like sawmills — which robbed the land and the Cree people — are now creating power, not waste. As the community describes it on their website

> Our energy system is proof that energy can be generated as if communities and the environment mattered, unlike megaprojects, for instance. It is proof also that the philosophies and traditional practices of aboriginal peoples are relevant to the establishment of modern sustainable communities.[7]

Most of the residences in Oujé-Bougoumou are single family homes, with occasional blocks of multi-family dwellings. In some ways, this is unlike other sites we visited where many people sharing smaller square footage is a path to greener living. Here at Oujé-Bougoumou, providing home ownership as a means toward achieving financial independence is a founding value — a value that contributes to the overall social sustainability of Oujé-Bougoumou. In designing the village in adherence to the goal of financial viability, there was an explicit effort to provide adequate and affordable housing. Critical of the situation for vast numbers of aboriginal people in Canada who live without adequate housing and are dependant on government programs that don't meet their needs, the designers of Oujé-Bougoumou wanted to do things differently. They decided to implement their own housing program which provides affordable,

Donald Fosker

Fig. 1.12: *Oujé-Bougoumou Residential Buildings.*

comfortable and energy-efficient housing to all community members with an emphasis on local labor for the construction and conformity with the natural terrain to reduce costs of water/sewer infrastructure. Doing so is one of the greatest successes of this community and an exemplar for social and economic sustainability.

Walking along the streets at Oujé-Bougoumou, it is clear that this village is not a perfect place. The walk along the sandy shore of the breathtaking Lake Opemiska, with its red waters and multiple bays and inlets that fade into a blue grey mist, was somewhat obscured by the litter gathered along the beach. However, the occasional boarded up building, periodic drone of an all-terrain-vehicle and roadside trash pale in comparison to what was going right here. The sidewalks, playing fields and playgrounds teemed with kids on bikes, on foot, in groups and by themselves. They were all speaking Cree to each other, but slipped into English or French when they greeted us. The community buildings were full and active, resonating with a happy buzz. The well-trodden paths between houses testify to the neighborliness cultivated here. Indeed, it seems that Oujé-Bougoumou has most definitely met their goal laid out in their vision statement:

> If we could structure our new village and our new environment in such a way as to meet all of the varied needs of our people then the result would be a

place which produced healthy, secure, confident and optimistic people who felt good about themselves and able to take on any challenges which may confront us.[8]

Maintaining Community through Sustainable Design + Interaction

The Oujé-Bougoumou People spent years of forced relocation, suffering through the scattering and fragmentation of their community. With every relocation, some people would settle away from the group or join other communities. Alongside the systematic destruction of the environment by clearcutting, mining and their attendant industries which interfered with the people's ability to live off of the land in traditional ways, this fracturing of community began to take its toll on the preservation of culture. By developing their permanent village, the people have been able to sustain language, knowledge and cultural practices. Once again the Oujé-Bougoumou Cree have a place to call home within their vast expanse of native lands, much of which is still being occupied and pillaged for profit by non-Aboriginal people. Having a neighborhood, a village of their own provides a means for connecting with one another and for passing down the stories and lessons of their ancestors to the next generation. This has brought social sustainability to the Oujé-Bougoumou People.

At the same time, this community itself is contributing to environmental sustainability. It does so through its green designs, incorporation of high-tech building innovations and sustainable activities of everyday life as well as through the political activism that building the community initiated. It also contributes to environmental sustainability because the very fact of preserving community and culture means preserving knowledge about environmental stewardship that is essential to greening all facets of contemporary society. In order to live sustainably, we all need to live within the carrying capacity of our region, and no one knows land like people who have lived there for centuries. There is much knowledge to be gained from indigenous science — as Paul Hawken calls it, "an observational science recorded in myths, stories, teachings and, in particular, language."[9] When thousands of languages become endangered or extinct, knowledge as to how to live within that language area's carrying capacity is lost forever. Oujé-Bougoumou is one among many communities around the world where the danger of this extinction has been removed — a reversal which benefits all of us.

Twin Oaks, while its roots are more recent, nonetheless also has important lessons to transmit through an approach to community that is inseparable from environmental, economic and social sustainability. We found that shared ideals, identities, resources and even income do not make a sustainable community: People do. People interacting together, making decisions together and creating a cultural and social life that draws upon history, culture, and the unique context of their lands and lives can be sustained over time. As Twin Oaks reveals, explicit green design and architecture principles are not one-way arrows to the creation of a sustainable community, but these work hand in hand with the commitment of the people living there. Twin Oaks, similarly to other communities we visited, requires ongoing commitments that extend to everyday actions to share resources and work to meet the needs of many. This form of action does not occur easily within larger North American ideals that privilege individualism and nuclear families and reward personal success. What makes Twin Oaks and other communities able to sustain themselves over time is ongoing collaboration — in conflict and agreement — among the members who live there. It is a chosen community, born of commitment and sustained by action.

Living Green through Cohousing

THANKS IN PART TO HILLARY RODHAM CLINTON'S BOOK of the same title, "It takes a village ..." became a familiar adage in the 1990s. Derived from the proverb "It takes a village to raise a child," the phrase became popularly used to critique the isolation and alienation of contemporary culture. It harkens back to both imagined and real times where people weren't expected to navigate the seas of child-rearing with just one or two parents at the helm. Thirty years earlier, these same critiques inspired a housing revolution.

In 1967, Bodil Graae published "Children Should Have One Hundred Parents" and helped launch a movement aimed at rebuilding tight-knit communities and giving people back villages within which to raise their children. Bodil Graae, along with the architect Jan Gudmand-Hoyer, is credited with igniting the concept of cohousing. Individually and then ultimately together with many others, they made Denmark the birthplace of a new way of developing housing that integrates community at every step. Instead of envisioning isolated units, cohousing starts with a group of people and builds habitations that encourage interconnectedness. Cohousing communities are usually designed as attached or single-family homes along one or more pedestrian streets or clustered around a courtyard. A common house is typically the heart of a cohousing community, providing space for gathering and the site of shared amenities.

In the early 1980s, architects Kathryn McCamant and Charles Durrett brought the cohousing concept to the US with the publication of their book *Cohousing: A Contemporary Approach to Housing Ourselves*, and since then the concept has expanded throughout North America. Cohousing communities vary in size, averaging 20 to 40 households. They range from small, very close-knit communities to more loosely connected groups of people residing near one another. They all share a commitment to a collaborative decision-making process and to residents designing, maintaining and managing their housing themselves. While also emphasizing communalism, unlike communes, cohousing is not based in a model of complete resource sharing. In contrast, most cohousing communities are based on ownership models and the degree of shared responsibilities varies enormously across communities. Initially conceptualized with the challenges of raising children in mind, cohousing soon became an important option for the challenges of aging, and the number of elder cohousing communities is growing.[1]

Cohousing as Green Living

The values of community and interconnectedness sparked the cohousing movement. That these values provide people with an alternative way of taking care of themselves and each other makes cohousing also a very good way of taking care of the planet. In many ways cohousing is by its very nature a practice of living green, and a large part of that is due to its focus on community.

By design, cohousing communities house more people on less land and thus tend to have a smaller ecological footprint. They are designed to have high density. Because some resources and spaces are shared, each individual living in cohousing tends to require less than individuals living in mainstream housing. Things as simple as a shared toy chest or as significant as an available guest room allow people to have more but own less. In his study of cohousing as models of sustainable communities, Graham Meltzer argues that elements of the community dynamic created by cohousing create pro-environmental practices. Citing the disconnect between how much people claim to care about the environment (a lot) and how much people actual live their lives in ways that benefit the environment (very little), Meltzer sought to understand how intentional communities like cohousing can bridge that gap and help people live closer to their espoused values of environmentalism.[2]

Close proximity, close social connections, sharing resources, building social trust and sense of community — these are ways cohousing promotes sustainability. One of the things that make cohousing unique from other communities where strong bonds may also be present, according to Meltzer, is the intentionality of cohousing and the fact that members participate fully in the design and ongoing manipulation of their built environment. With environmental values at the fore, cohousers can build their communities in ways which explicitly meet high environmental standards and also in ways which they know will help them live by and maintain those standards.

From sharing tools to sharing cars, from living in smaller spaces to transmitting common values, our experiences with people living in cohousing taught us many ways in which cohousing encourages green living both purposefully and tacitly. In this chapter, we showcase two sister cohousing communities located in the Washington DC metropolitan area: Takoma Village Community (TVC) and Eastern Village Cohousing (EVC). While every cohousing community is unique, the stories we tell here resonate with the contributions cohousing everywhere is making to the sustainability of our planet.

Planning and Building Together

A defining feature of cohousing is that residents are involved in the process of a community's development from its very inception. Both TVC and EVC were co-created by future residents and developers. In describing her involvement with Takoma Village, Ann Zabaldo talked about becoming a community in the two years prior to completion of the site; future residents hashed out the details of what would become their neighborhood and began knowing each other, caring about each other and accommodating the visions that each held. In the case of Takoma Village and Eastern Village, the visions being transformed into living spaces included an established commitment to environmental sustainability. Future residents were committed to integrating green design features throughout the built environment and, because they were committed to paying for these features, the development partners could build confidently, knowing that residents would buy the final product.

One of the first ways that the developers and future residents built green was to pay close attention to location: the context and culture of the neighborhood. Completed in 2001, Takoma Village was the Washington DC area's first cohousing community. It's an urban infill development located in the Takoma community area that has a long and vibrant political and cultural history — one that resonates with the mostly liberal residents of Takoma Park and Eastern Village.

In 1907 the Seventh Day Adventist Church relocated from Michigan and became the largest employer and most influential cultural force in the Takoma area. During the social and cultural revolution of the 1950s and 1960s, hippies found the vegetarian lifestyle and communal spirit of the Adventists very attractive. The community supported anti-war and anti-nuclear demonstrations, fostered environmentalism and pioneered recycling programs. In the 1960s town members protested a proposed freeway that would have bisected the town and destroyed the old business district. In the 1970s they opposed building a new parking garage to serve the metro, hoping to encourage walking. The mostly liberal group of cohousers who reside at Takoma and Eastern Village mesh well with the non-profit organizations, political activists, writers, academics, artists, gardeners, journalists, musicians and dancers that have all been attracted to the principles held by Takoma residents throughout the years.

Takoma Village Community's central courtyard, known by the residents as The Green, opens into a residential area a few blocks from all that Takoma and its surrounding area has to offer. It's just a few blocks to the Takoma Community Center and one more block to downtown where transportation, restaurants and cultural amenities are available. There are a library, post office, a public transportation hub, two car-sharing options and multiple bicycle and pedestrian routes as well as locally owned small businesses and restaurants nearby. Downtown Takoma Park contains vegetarian restaurants and caterers, a natural foods co-op store, a large Buddhist community, yoga practices, midwives and massage therapists. It is home to a weekly Farmer's Market requiring that all products

Fig. 2.1: *Takoma Village Community Cohousing.*

be produced within 125 miles of the village, an annual House and Garden Tour and an annual free folk festival that celebrates local and international art and culture.

Takoma Village Community consists of 43 apartments and townhouses. Three-story townhouses line the entrance walkway that leads to the main shared house and individual apartments. The townhouses are architecturally designed in the federal style popular in the District of Columbia. At TVC, these are wooden structures with front, ground-level porches and rear decks. The townhouses range from one to four bedrooms. A 4,800 square foot common building houses an exercise room, playroom, kitchen and dining room, two guest rooms, an office, a workshop, a laundry room, a music room and a living room as well as several individual apartments. Elective common meals take place here as well as informal gatherings and celebrations. The residential units each face a common green space and courtyard where tables and chairs mingle with kids' bicycles and scooters.

Fig. 2.2: *Eastern Village Community Entrance.*

Designing green also meant that the people who developed TVC decided to pay close attention to the materials they used in the buildings themselves. Knowing that the future residents were committed to sustainable building materials, they selected materials based (among other criteria) on health effects and environmental sustainability. The paint, adhesives and sealants used throughout are low-VOC (volatile organic compounds, which are common in most of construction materials and have documented ill effects on health and the environment); the buildings are framed using sustainably harvested lumber and low-toxicity wood preservatives; recycled content is used in both insulation and carpeting and efficient lighting and appliances are used throughout. Heating and cooling systems are made efficient through the use of geothermal or ground-source heat pumps with smart thermostats. As a result of all of these features, Takoma Village is a high performance building case study for the US Department of Energy.

Completed and occupied in 2004, Eastern Village Cohousing (EVC) is an adaptive reuse of a long unused office building. It includes 56 units of cohousing and 11 units of commercial space all located inside two adjacent four-story low-rise buildings connected via a common area. The common space includes an exercise room, guest rooms, living room, dining room, playroom for young children and another for older children and teens, yoga room, library and workshop. There are green common spaces, both at ground level onto which the units face and on the roof, where a vegetated green roof is the crowning feature of EVC. The roof includes garden space, walkways, a gazebo and a children's play area. Trellises with both deciduous and evergreen vines are located on the front façade of the building adding to seasonal heating and cooling gain. Located close to TVC, EVC includes access to all of the amenities of Takoma Park and, like its neighbor, is an eminently walkable community. The courtyard of EVC was formerly a parking lot.

In the case of EVC, the (soon-to-be) residents intentionally and explicitly designed the built environment to meet the standards for LEED certification, becoming one of the few residential buildings to attain a silver certificate from the USGBC. EVC has several significant environmentally-friendly features including geothermal heating, native planting, low-emitting materials and the vegetated roof used to enhance cooling in what is a very hot climate. It is an award winning construction project. In 2006, EVC was a recipient of the Green Roof Award for Excellence given by Green Roofs for Healthy Cities. In 2005, it received a design award for multi-use buildings by *Environmental Design + Construction (ED + C)*, a magazine covering the green building industry; more recently it has been recognized by the Smart Growth Alliance and the National Association of Home Builders for its exceptional green construction.

When we arrived at EVC and TVC for our interviews with residents we were immediately drawn into the uniquely green and community-centric auras that these communities have cultivated. The narrow entrance of each community transported us from an active, urban world to a quiet green space with multiple residential doorways at each side and a focal entranceway in front. It was late spring, and flowers spilled over the tops of the wooden boxes affixed to the balconies at EVC while a perfectly

Fig. 2.3: *Research Team Arrives with Kids in Tow.*

Helen Firzsimmons

pink beech tree overflowing with leaves gracefully brushed the common green at TVC. Inside the boundaries of the communities, the air felt clean as open windows circulated the spring breeze, and the lushness of landscaping tempered the heat of the day.

Besides ourselves, we arrived with a research assistant, a photographer and two small children. Anywhere else such an entourage would be an impossibility on a research trip, but here, the community welcomed us: the kids played dress-up and zookeeper in well-appointed playrooms; those of us who weren't interviewing found comfortable places to sit, relax and supervise the play. In this warm

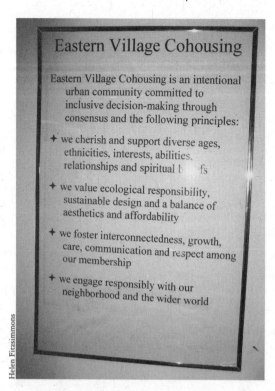

Helen Fitzsimmons

Fig. 2.4: *Eastern Village Value Statement.*

atmosphere we enjoyed a day of talking with residents, and it was in these dialogues that we learned how cohousing enables people to live in environmentally and socially sustainable ways.

Community Living as Green Living

Environmental sustainability was literally built into the foundations of Takoma Village and Eastern Village. Although designed at different times with divergent technologies available to them, each incorporated green building design features and technologies from low-tech landscape design, proximity to transportation or the inclusion of a shared compost to water and heating building innovations such as the green roof built at EVC. However, it is perhaps not the bricks and mortar of the sites which are their most sustainable features. Instead, it is the sustainability provided by the community that is most significant here. As Takoma Village resident and long-time cohousing activist Ann said

It's great the buildings are green, but buildings in and of themselves aren't sustainable. What really makes sustainability happen is the community. The community is really the nexus where people's values get to be lived out — and cohousing provides an opportunity to have that happen. There are features within this community [which], for instance, because of the nature of sharing, make sustainability possible.

Sociologists understand values to be the abstract standards that define ideal principles: they provide a compass for what is considered wrong and right and a general outline for behavior. In traditional societies, values held by communities of people can be highly similar. As societies grow more complex, values are much more likely to diverge and conflict and, as we are all acutely aware, full-scale wars can rage over differing value systems.

Even within families or groups that share values, many find it hard to live in accordance with those values because of the competing messages about wrong and right that circulate throughout the larger culture. For instance, generally in North America there is a high value on consumption: having the best and newest thing is a symbol of one's membership in dominant society. This is a value that competes with the value of environmental sustainability with its emphasis on simplifying, on reusing and recycling and limiting consumption. For many who hold strong values of environmental sustainability in the abstract, actually living according to those values in a society that encourages the opposite can be a challenge.

Raising kids to adhere to values of sustainability can be even more chal-

Fig. 2.5: *Cohousing's Next Generation Gardening.*

lenging. In his study of cohousing, Graham Meltzer described the ways in which children growing up in cohousing are socialized to ascribe to values of environmentalism and learn how to put those values into practice. With cohousing, primary agents of socialization expand from just the nuclear family, school and media to include an extended community who share similar values. Thus children aren't just learning about sustainability from parents but from each of the multi-generational members of their larger community.

Part of cohousing, we found, is not a top-down ideology to live with less, but practical solutions for living in modern times in ways that reduce individual expenditures (economic and otherwise) but not the things that enhance one's life. Takoma and Eastern Villages, like many other cohousing communities, include a handful of values that serve as founding principles. Each individual is supposed to live according to these values and to help others do so as well. One of these values is environmental sustainability. We were told time and time again that one of the unique qualities of living in these communities is the way in which people feel individually encouraged and compelled to live according to this value.

One couple we interviewed at Eastern Village described this idea of living with people who share similar values of environmental sustainability as one of the benefits of living there. Joe said

> The fact [is] that there is a commitment, I think, to live your lives in environmentally healthy ways. Even though, inevitably, everybody falls short of the ideals, the shared commitment is a pretty nice thing.

His wife added "it certainly is nice to live with people who have shared values about the environment." This couple saw shared values as a way to increase one's awareness of environmental issues and elicit new ways of living environmentally sustainable existences. For them, being a part of the design of EVC with its emphasis on sustainability opened their eyes to new ideas, such as the negative impacts built environments are having on the planet and the solutions available to counter those impacts. As Joe said

> So, living together with a group of people like that I mean you all kind of help each other see things that one or the other of you hadn't seen in the first place. And you keep going to a slightly higher level.

In the day to day experiences of many members of these communities, living in close proximity to people with commitments to green living is both an inspiration and a way to learn. From recycling and composting to energy efficient appliances, residents discuss the mundane ways that commitments to living green get passed along in a close-knit community. In Takoma Village, Bill described

> Since we've been here there's a composting thing in the back, and I've never composted ... But it's so easy. It's easy because someone else has volunteered to take care of it. I don't think I'd do it if I had to go out there and go through the steps ... I wouldn't have done it had I not lived here.

At EVC Joan said

> Yeah, we didn't know about Energy Star appliances, and of course we have them and we would always get them. Because of the experience of living here I would always be much more aware.

At EVC Amy said

> We've been very big on recycling and conserving. Like the environmental part we always thought we were really in tune with, but living here, there's just so much more that we're in tune with.

The possibility of living according to one's values is reinforced in cohousing in a day to day fashion, as people respond to the peer pressure of others living sustainably and, perhaps most importantly, as the support of community enables people to share the work involved in living green. As Bill remarked, it is the fact that there are other people doing some of the work that allows him to contribute his piece to the overall puzzle of sustainability.

It is this form of communal effort that maintains sustainable practices at these cohousing communities. Here, commitment to community means pooling resources, and there are multiple ways that this helps people live in greener ways. As Ann described it

Bill Bank

Fig. 2.6: *Cohousers at a
Meeting.*

I don't think we get very far when we ask people to give up stuff. So, instead of giving up, I just pool my money or pool my resources with other people, and I get infinitely more. Like the hot tub for example: I can't afford it on my own, but together we have one!

On a practical level, pooling resources has meant the ability to afford to be green. Ann described ways in which members were able to incorporate expensive green design features into Takoma Village as a result of pooling resources — possibilities that would have excluded many individuals if they were focusing on their own, single family dwellings. For an individual to put in a geothermal system may not be cost effective; using timber from renewable resources can be prohibitively expensive for many individuals. But by pooling resources residents of EVC could afford to do both. And it's not just building material; cohousers regularly bulk purchase everything from food to screen doors and are able to get better quality (and often environmentally-friendly) products for less cost as a result.

Perhaps most importantly, people living in cohousing can, as individuals, live with less. From not having to have a car to having houses that are smaller than average for North America, by pooling resources cohousing enables people to have less without sacrificing quality of life. As Ann described, it's more feasible and possible to live in smaller houses because they aren't really giving anything up: the common house has guest rooms, an exercise room and play room. So, each individual doesn't need extra room in their own house to have those things.

In Meltzer's research, he found that people living in cohousing owned 24% fewer freezers, washers and dryers and 75% fewer mowers than they did before living in cohousing. The people we spoke with described an informal network of sharing that enabled a similar scaling down of material possessions. Tools, bicycles, printers, computers, toys and clothes were all passed down, lent and borrowed. More formally, an internet community message board allowed for such sharing, and both TVC and EVC have areas where people can leave stuff they are getting rid of so other people can browse if they are in need of something.

And having less stuff, of course, contributes to sustainable living. Considering the resources that are put into the manufacture of any given material item, transportation and storage before it even gets to the user and then the resources involved in disposing of it, each time a person manages to borrow, share or get something from a neighbor instead of buying it new, the planet is a little bit better off. Cohousing accelerates this possibility.

Car sharing is another key way cohousing contributes to sustainability. Whereas it is not uncommon for households to have more than one car in North America, at both EVC and TVC there is fewer than one car per household. This is possible because of the communities' locations; residents were committed to building close to public transportation. But also members share cars, give each other rides and help out with errands that may require occasional car use (for which most people, lacking community support, are likely to own a car).

A couple we spoke with at EVC described the multiple benefits of not owning a car: it has made a difference in their lives in terms of health and well-being and also made them feel good in terms of their contribution to the planet.

Feels so much healthier in every way. It also makes
you recognize we could really as a nation cut way
down, and we just don't do it. We don't seriously
think about adapting our lives to meet the things we
say we believe in.

We have found that there are multiple ways that these communities,
and we suspect the many other cohousing communities springing up
around the world, are contributing to human health and well-being. One
of the major ways this is being conceptualized in cohousing is a capacity
to improve *aging in place*: that is, the ability for people to live at home
longer, before having (or without ever having) to move to a long-term
care facility of some kind. One of the residents we spoke with at TVC
has been active in the senior cohousing movement, and she described
some of the ways cohousing can better address the needs of elders.

Older people can actually live longer in their houses
and they age in place in community as opposed to
aging in place isolated. So that's another sustainability feature. It also means that even in intergenerational
cohousing, seniors could get together and hire a
caregiver if they need to that can come in and help
four or five families. This is really important because
as the population ages, we are going to have more
people being supported by fewer people ... and it
will be a lot easier to deliver services to people who
live in a group as opposed to people who are spread
out all over.

Just as cohousing provides a village within which people could more
easily raise their children, it similarly reproduces that support network
that enables people to more easily meet the challenges of aging. Living
in the midst of supportive community may also ease the challenges of
living with illnesses or disabilities. In response to whether or not living
in Takoma Park affected her health and well-being, Ann answered

Absolutely. I mean, you can see I have a disability. I don't think I would have anywhere near the quality of life that I have if I didn't live in this kind of community that's been so supportive of me. I just wouldn't have it.

Ann went on to describe the give and take of community support: she picks up a neighbor's kid at school, she takes care of people's dogs, she helps people with the administrative jobs of everyday life. And, in describing the mutuality of support it's clear that as both the giver and receiver of help she is buoyed. In this way, the everyday experiences of living in cohousing communities in and of themselves can be a positive contribution to well-being.

Takoma Village also formally contributes to the health and well-being of its members through its Care Team. The Care Team organizes meals, gets people to the doctor or whatever else they may need if they are faced with illness, deaths in the family, new babies or any issue where ongoing care could be required. These practices are not only useful for aging bodies but for anyone living with a life-long disability or experiencing an acute or chronic illness. Anyone might need the support of a grocery run, a social visit or a shared meal.

Takoma and Eastern Villages also contribute to health specifically through their use of green building materials. For instance, in describing the green features of the building where she lives Amy said

So, thinking about what kind of products are going into my body or being emitted from the furniture or whatever. That makes me feel a lot better about day to day life.

Finally, we found that health is not only about one's physical well-being but is about emotional sustenance as well. Many of the residents we spoke with discussed the unforeseen benefits of both intergenerational living and a more social existence. Bill, for example, talked about his initial worry about living around young

Fig. 2.7: *Ann Zabaldo with Neighbor, Robbin Phelps.*

Bill Bank

Bill Bank

Fig. 2.8: *TVC Residents and Neighbors After Tree Planting Project with Casey Trees* .

children. He has found, to his surprise, that being in control of when and in what ways he spends time with kids is uplifting. "The best part is that I can decide when I have had enough," he laughed.

We experienced firsthand a community party at Takoma Village for Leap Year (Upside Down Day as the residents called it). During this potluck children were invited to perform in a variety show and, while many adults enjoyed this presentation, other sat amongst themselves, working on a large format puzzle with thousand of pieces that had been in progress for months in the common room. Amongst all party participants, old and young, there seemed to be profound confidence and well-being — a sense of belonging.

Actions that Sustain

What cohousing teaches us about environmentalism and sustainability is the simple lesson that a built environment cannot maintain its sustainable properties unless the people who live there are dedicated to working together to do so. We do not want to imply that this is an easy nor seamless effort. In fact, we found, that one of the main obstacles to community sustainability is the time and human energy involved in reaching consensus or engaging in shared management of a community.

What we saw at Takoma Village and Eastern Village is the way in which community is a key element of sustainability: environmental, social and economic. Community can help to create sustainable living in the first place by contributing ideas, values, expertise and financial capital to the project of creating green built environments. This is what happened at Eastern Village and Takoma Village: the community collectively envisioned, designed and built environments that were green. Individuals committed to creating green built environments would have a hard time accomplishing as much as the folks at EVC and TVC were able to do collectively. As one resident said about her time at EVC

> You evolve. Most people here [in the wider community] have not done what we've done. We've done a lot of moving to the next stage. Unfortunately, if every human being has to start from the beginning and go as long as it's taken us to go through all of that stuff ...

By working together ideas were brighter, dreams were bigger and the capacity to realize them was financially achievable. Once built, it was the community itself that enabled the maintenance of living green. As one member of EVC said, "You can have the most beautiful, color-coded recycling center that you want, but if people don't use it, it's hardly a sustainable feature." Community connections are what help. The interactional features of community — trust, commitment, sharing of knowledge, work and resources — create an ethic which supports living green in these communities. It doesn't mean that people always do the right thing, but that it is much easier for them to make that choice. Barriers to living green (like lack of support, hyperindividualism or lack of time) are lifted when actions sustain community connection, access to technologies and knowledge, and beliefs in the need to do so.

Part 2

Social Justice and Sustainability

An Alternative for Los Angeles

IN AN ALLEY IN DOWNTOWN LOS ANGELES between First and Second streets and connecting Bimini and Vermont, a crowd gathered around the energetic figure of Lois Arkin. Gesturing to the cracked asphalt, Lois said, "This is what some people call an alley. I call this a promenade."

Fig. 3.1: *LA Ecovillage.*

LA Ecovillage

It was a hot day, and the sweet, acrid stench of urine emanated from the asphalt. Diesel trucks could be heard, a helicopter circled nearby, the back of a strip mall spewed out exhaust and cars drove through the alley vying for sneaky routes past traffic-choked Vermont Avenue. Nearby, a man lay on the sidewalk, curled into the fetal position, faced away from us and protectively cradling his bundle of belongings.

But all of this is not what Lois saw: she saw something else entirely. Her gesturing arms, exuberant words and big smile excitedly painted a picture of *the promenade*: asphalt turned into green space, parking lot into a tot play area, fruit trees planted through the center of tables around which community members and neighbors gather to chat. And, when Lois paints such a picture, you've got to believe it's going to happen. Dreamer and pragmatist undaunted by politics, bureaucracy and the tedium of getting things done, Lois Arkin is the founder of Los Angeles Ecovillage with a history of bringing outrageous green visions to life.

Ecovillage is the term used to describe a diverse array of intentional communities designed with a commitment to social, economic and environmental sustainability. Similar to cohousing, ecovillages are also intentional communities where community connectedness is cultivated and nurtured. Quality time with neighbors, friends and family are built in to village life through close proximity to leisure, civic and recreational activities. However, whereas cohousing emerges to meet a variety of social needs, ecovillages are explicitly designed to meet environmental goals.[1] Ecological in philosophy, ecovillages strive to live lightly on the planet, giving back as much as they take away; they do so in ways that ensure the wellness of future generations to come. Such an emphasis on intergenerational justice lies at the heart of sustainable ecology and the founding ideals of ecovillages. The ecovillage concept is continually evolving as urban, rural, small- and medium-sized intentional communities self-identified as ecovillages figure out better ways to meet the challenges of contemporary society. As Lois Arkin observed, ecovillages will emerge in different ways depending on the problems faced by particular communities.

LA Ecovillage lies in the heart of a working class, multiethnic neighborhood in inner city Los Angeles. Built as an intentional community, it brings people together through its workshops, bicycle clinics, informal gathering spaces, community events and meetings. In Los Angeles, urban disconnection, reliance on cars and intersecting social, political and economic disenfranchisement all led LA Ecovillage to emerge as a demonstration of car-free high quality living on less land, of greening small urban spaces and of contributing toward sustainable affordability of ecologically friendly lifestyles.

Beginnings

On March 3rd, 1991 an African American man named Rodney King was brutally beaten by four white police officers from the Los Angeles Police Department. To many, this marked business as usual for a department considered rife with racism, human rights' violations and heavy-handed policing. To others, it marked necessary force in a city considered to be riddled with the worst gang violence anywhere in the US. Regardless of interpretation, what was undeniably unique about the beating of this man by these police was that it was all captured on videotape.

An immediate and intense response arose to the public witnessing of the beating of Rodney King. The police officers involved were charged with assault with a deadly weapon and use of excessive force. The trial was moved out of Los Angeles to a predominantly white suburb north of the city, and on April 29, 1992 the officers were each acquitted by an all-white jury.

The lack of prosecution of these officers was deemed to be so unjust and racist that it unleashed what is considered by many to be the largest uprising in US history. The Rodney King riots or uprisings as they are alternatively called swept through inner city Los Angeles. For three days people took to the streets, and the ensuing violence brought into sharp relief the institutionalized racism, economic and social injustices that plagued the United States. In the end, 55 people were killed and more than 2,300 were injured. More than 1,100 buildings were damaged or destroyed. In Koreatown, businesses were looted, cars overturned and strip malls burned down.

On a street immediately behind one of those burnt down strip malls, in the ashes of social unrest and community breakdown, the Los Angeles Ecovillage (LAEV) took root. LAEV founder Lois Arkin had been involved in community formation initiatives for some time, and in 1980 she founded the non-profit organization Cooperative Resources and Services Project (CRSP) as a resource center for small ecological cooperative communities. CRSP and Arkin had been thinking about finding a place for developing an ecovillage. Initially, their sights were set on a landfill five miles from downtown, but after the Rodney King uprisings Lois decided the most important thing she could do was to stay and build right where she was.

Central Los Angeles is a set of racially and ethnically diverse neighborhoods, disproportionately low-income and African American. The area shoulders an unfair burden of environmental injustices (e.g., car congestion and pollution), and by extension, higher rates of childhood asthma. The development of LAEV is not only a story of an ecovillage; it is part of an environmental justice movement. Environmental justice is defined as a "local, grassroots, or 'bottom-up' community reaction to external threats to the health of the community, which have been shown to disproportionately affect people of color and low-income neighborhoods."[2] Lois Arkin described the development of LAEV as part of "healing an inner city neighborhood."

The first challenge LAEV's founders faced was how to begin to develop trust amongst neighbors who were steadfastly fearful of one another. They started by organizing a community brunch. They invited all of the neighborhood children, and they gave them tastes of different kinds of fruit. Then they asked them which were their favorites? Which trees would they like to plant? The kids picked trees, gave them names, drew pictures of them. Later, as holes were being dug, the kids tapped the ground, telling the critters underground that a tree was coming. When the trees were planted they held hands encircling the new additions to the neighborhood and talked about the future they symbolized, the fruit they would bear and how it meant their moms would no longer have to buy fruit.

In the planting of the trees, the founders of LAEV and others who joined from within the community were enacting what has come to be an important part of LAEV: the making of connections among ecological, social and economic systems. Bringing people together focused on social sustainability: creating connections and bonds between people and rebuilding

Fig. 3.2: *LAEV Doorway with Sustainable Wood and Double Glazed Windows.*

LA Ecovillage

trust among groups that had become suspicious of each other. The planting of trees highlighted ecological commitment — the need to create environmental sustainability by transforming the concrete neighborhood into something greener. And, finally, by choosing edible trees, the founders emphasized the economic value of living green — that what is environmentally sustainable can also have immediate economic benefit. To the kids living in this neighborhood, the availability of free fruit hanging from trees was of more than symbolic value. Today, LAEV estimates that they have planted over 100 fruit-producing trees in the two block radius that they call home.

In order to create a community that met the specific needs of the people living there, the founders of LAEV (locals themselves) gathered their neighbors together to find out what their biggest concerns were. Crime topped the list. While this wasn't surprising, especially in light of the recent uprising, it was frustrating to the founders who viewed crime as a symptom of the larger issue of community breakdown, not as its cause. But, as Lois has said, "You've got to meet people where they're at." So they talked about crime. And they all agreed to foster better connections and encourage more participation in the neighborhood by encouraging people to do one simple thing: to introduce themselves to one person and to find out that person's name. If every person did this just once a week, community bonds and trust amongst neighbors would be stronger. They also practiced what Lois Arkin calls *positive gossip* — telling people good things about other people. A year later when LAEV had another neighborhood forum to find out from people what their biggest issues were, crime appeared only on page three and only as an afterthought.

In the early 1990s LAEV was being established with very little money. As Lois described it they were "using only passion, love and energy to create an ecovillage." The brunches, potlucks, meetings, tree plantings and other community events marked the beginning of LAEV; they were creating a sense of community before there was an actual centralized residence to house LAEV. The first three years of LAEV occurred in the streets — talking to people, interacting, playing. "We are a neighborhood in the process of becoming an intentional community by virtue of our prior residential choices," wrote Arkin in the early days of LAEV. Neighborhood cannot be imported, you have to begin from working, playing and interacting together.[3] It's a local, grass-roots effort.

At the time of the founding, Lois resided in a fourplex at the corner of White House Place and Bimini that was owned by the Los Angeles Unified School District. She had moved there from a fourplex next door that had been demolished to make way for White House Primary Center, a public elementary school. The corner fourplex became the first site of LAEV activities. Arkin and her non-profit CRSP were located there, and soon a community garden flourished. Another LAEV founder Esfandiar Abbazzi began to work with the new school, bringing children over to garden, and the site was transformed into an outdoor classroom. "Mr. Plant" (as Esfandiar became known) was a well-loved figure, and his environmental curriculum was a valuable addition to the elementary school. In 1996 two more ecovillagers, Anna Noriega and Jeff Davis, started a library in the corner fourplex, and kids started coming over for that as well.

In 1997, LAEVs ethic of environmental justice was put to the test: the school district informed the community that they had decided to demolish the building and gave Lois, CRSP, the library and other tenants 30 days to vacate. A massive effort to save the corner ensued. Members of Congress, senators, city council members, directors and staff of non-profits, teachers, professors, principals and many others wrote letters, made phone calls, and protested in the streets against this decision. Parents of kids who went to the school as well as many other residents also expressed their outrage. After reprieves, further threats and various flurries of protests, the outdoor classroom and library eventually closed down. But, in the time that lapsed LAEV had successfully bought a nearby building and used it as the new center of action.

Across the street from the corner fourplex, a 40-unit courtyard-style apartment building came up for sale in 1996. By now this neighborhood had not only lived through riots, but Los Angeles had suffered through the major Northridge earthquake and prices were low. CRSP bought the building for $500,000 with cash raised through their ecological revolving loan fund, a community development loan fund which accepts loans from those interested in socially and environmentally responsible investments.

The building was half empty, and LAEV was committed to not displacing anyone involuntarily: a commitment they have honored. Further, they continue to be committed to keeping the units very affordable; for those that stayed, leaving becomes more of a financial hardship all the time. As a result, there have been dwindling numbers of residents at LAEV who are not part of the intentional community but have been here since before it was an ecovillage. These residents continue to dwell here with varying levels of connectedness to the ecovillage. In 1999 CRSP bought the adjacent eight-unit apartment building, and today the two buildings form the heart of LAEV — though its borders extend beyond this heart.

Intentional Community at LA Ecovillage

A warm breeze blew through the living room at LAEV. Three sets of French doors, painted green and standing open, lead out into the back yard on one end, and another set of French doors opens into the front garden at the other. These doors make this room feel like it's inside and outside simultaneously; the smells from the back and front gardens mingled with the slightly musty smell of the old building that houses LAEV. Comfortable furniture has been set up to encourage the formation of spontaneous gatherings; there are couches, soft stuffed chairs and a huge coffee table. This room also has a piano and a fish tank where two orange fish played circular games of chase.

The front half of the room marks the entrance to LAEV, and a big table provides pamphlets of information on various causes, projects linked to the ecovillage and other political and social issues deemed important by those who left them. Above this table, a bulletin board serves as a communication and announcement board; to it were pinned various items of interest interspersed with cut-out cartoons, mostly lampooning George W. and Dick Cheney. Mailboxes are in this room, and a couple of chairs are facing out the front door, providing another place for spontaneous gathering.

Opportunities for connecting with others highlight an intentional characteristic of ecovillages: whereas most apartment buildings prioritize

Fig. 3.3: Organic Food Coop in LA Ecovillage Living Room.

LA Ecovillage

privacy over community and are built to reflect that, LAEV has worked to counter that built-in mechanism by creating shared spaces able to foster both intimacy and social vibrancy. They have transformed space and blurred distinctions of inside and outside as well as private and public. This maximizes the likelihood that people will interact and facilitates the building and maintenance of community.

Stepping outside the front entrance, you emerge into a small garden, the wrought-iron entry fence overflowing with bright pink bougainvillea. But to fully experience the gardens at LAEV, you must walk out the back doors into the common green space. There, a huge magnolia tree provides a centerpiece to a garden which includes over 25 fruit trees (apples, bananas, peaches, nectarines, pomegranates, plums and others), growing vegetables and flowers, a rabbit hutch (which used to also be a chicken coop) and an eclectic array of furniture and art made from found objects, salvaged materials and waste. The ground is springy with layers of brown mulch, and there is a messy chaotic beauty to the place.

There are 35 people who currently live at LAEV as part of the intentional community. In order to become a member, a rigorous process is required. Prospective members spend a long time getting to know LAEV and are the subject of several rounds of discussion and processing by current members. The aim of the membership policy is to ensure that everyone knows what they are getting into if and when they end up joining.

One of LA Ecovillage's missions is to be a demonstration project for how people can live higher quality lives in less space. Each of the units here is small. In the main building, most of the units are singles: they consist of a kitchen, bathroom and a main room that serves as everything else. When CRSP bought the building, there were families of four and five living in some of the single units. Not wanting to reproduce the unhealthy dynamic of overcrowding, they decided that for future residents the limit for a single would be two people. There are also some one bedroom units in the main building, and in the adjacent building there are one and two bedroom units. In these, LAEV instigated the policy that no fewer than two people could live in a one bedroom and no fewer than three people in a two bedroom. The intention has been to provide higher quality living in small spaces.

As with other intentional communities, one of the things that make the small spaces workable is the abundance of shared space. In addition to the living room and garden spaces, there is a common room at LAEV on the second floor of the main building. The common room has a kitchen, bathroom and a living room which houses comfy couches, a television and DVD/VCR player, a computer with Internet access and a printer. There is also a guest room available to visitors. The wide hallways form common spaces, and many people have decorated their doorways to incorporate this space with the others and encouraging social interaction.

In addition to the impromptu ways that people gather, there are weekly potlucks, weekly meetings and monthly work parties. Every member of the intentional community must commit to attending at least two out of three of these gatherings a month. Some of the people we spoke with describe attending only the minimum, while others describe participating much more. Those who are in the process of becoming members tend to attend as much as they can as this is the best way to get to know

Fig. 3.4: *LA Ecovillage Garden Party.*

LA Ecovillage

the community, the people in it and the expectations and responsibilities of becoming a resident.

Regardless of the level of participation in group events, members of LAEV are connected to their fellow members — for good or bad — by space, activities, meetings and some common interest in being a part of a grass-roots community. Some are committed to the racial and age diversity intentionally woven into the community, others feel strongly about reducing resource use and pollution associated with urban life and others believe that cohesion with neighbors can heal the stress, isolation, inequality and violence of contemporary life. But whatever their reason, people know the names, faces and even life stories of those they live among.

Car Free in LA

Twelve of us were on a tour of LAEV, and as we first moved outside Lois Arkin ushered us into the middle of the street. The street, a now-faded mosaic of color and design, has a painted symbol of a bicycle wheel in the center. It was to this circle, smack in the middle of the street that she herded us. Cars were approaching on either side, and there was a tentativeness among the tour goers — so ingrained is our impulse to get out of the way of approaching cars. Once we were all in the center of the circle, Lois continued to talk with us, looking up to smile and wave at the cars as they made their way around us. "Car retraining," she said, "We're used to getting out of their way. We're trying to get them used to getting out of ours."

Evidence of the destruction of the planet's ecosystem and increasing demand for the planet's natural resources are two of

Fig. 3.5: *Lois Arkin Car Retraining.*

LA Ecovillage

the many forces shaping the green building movement. Cars contribute to both of these forces. If current consumption rates continue, we will no longer be able to meet the needs of the present population without compromising the ability to meet the needs of future generations. Further, inner cities bear a disproportional burden of asthma caused by the pollution from cars as well as industrial production. Living car-free represents not only an environmental choice, but also an approach to improving public health, urban air pollution and heat effects and fighting environmental injustice.

Reducing reliance on cars and equalizing people's access to transportation are strong ethics at LAEV, which happens to be located near one of the most car-congested streets in the city. Commitment to living without cars, car sharing and having access to sidewalks and public transportation are central to LAEV's ethics. LAEV is located a two-minute walk from 20 bus lines and two metro lines, making it possible to live without car ownership. However, what makes living car-free even more possible is the strong bike culture of LAEV.

Virtually every one of the members of LAEV's intentional community has at least one bike. One of the apartments in the 40-unit main building (the least desirable one situated underneath the stairs) has been transformed into bike parking. The unit overflows with at least 25 bikes — and these are just the bikes that aren't out being ridden, aren't being kept inside people's apartments and aren't stored in an off-site garage that houses people's second and third bikes and bike parts. In describing the essential need to move away from car dependence Lois enumerated many of the problems with car reliance that we don't usually think about: it's not just fuel, it's the building of roads, it's the ways community breaks down when people get off their feet and off their bikes and into a car. Lois described how bikes bring forward features of social sustainability that lie at the heart of ecovillage life.

In 1998, an LA Ecovillager named Ron Milam founded a non-profit organization called the Los Angeles County Bike Coalition whose mission is to improve the bicycling environment and in so doing, improve overall quality of life in Los Angeles county. He described how living at LAEV provided support for his work.

Fig. 3.6: *Bike Kitchen.*

I always felt like the ecovillage was a place where my neighbors and my community really understood the work I was doing, were really supportive of the work I was doing and would often volunteer to help. One or two board members wound up living here. I remember once we had a story with a local news channel, and I put a call out — you know — 'I need bicyclist to come out to the river, channel 7's doing a story, who can come?' And I have this memory of maybe five or ten of us leaving from the ecovillage. So, it was really a supportive place for what I was doing. It was a place where professional and social blended into one.

Another LA Ecovillager and bike messenger named Jimmy began hosting fellow bicyclists for an evening of fixing bikes and sharing knowledge, passion and tools. They congregated in the apartment/bike room at LAEV, and as more people started showing up Jimmy would cook for the gathering and thus began the *bicycle kitchen*. As word spread, greater numbers of people of many ages and backgrounds started showing up for the DIY, learning, fixing and recycling bike phenomenon, and the group had to move to a larger venue. Today the bike kitchen is located in a storefront on Heliotrope drive, a short bike ride from LAEV. The night we visited was a Monday, which meant it was bitchen' night: a night open only to women where women teach other women how to fix their bikes and cheer one another on in the endeavor to prioritize bikes over cars as primary modes of transportation.

Other evidence of bike culture at LAEV include an art wall made of bike parts that was being constructed in the alley when we were visiting, a recent wedding between two ecovillagers whose only evidence on our visit was two bikes sporting white streamers and a sign which read "just married" on the backs, and endless stories of how people gave up their cars and picked up their bikes upon moving to LAEV.

A Permaculture Approach to Social Activism

Within permaculture, a permanent, sustainable, agricultural and human cultural environment is sought. At root here is the belief that everything — human, animal, mineral, vegetable — is connected. Permaculture infuses the landscape at LAEV: the common green space behind their buildings is a jungle of fruit trees, plants, vegetables and flowers all planted in circular patterns. Here biodiversity gives rise to natural insecticides and fertilizers. And woven into all of this ecological abundance are elements of the human world. Sculptures and salvaged wood proliferate, and literally woven in to the landscape is a loom stretched between two trees with recycled plastic bags acting as yarn; this is the work of the head of the gardening committee who also happens to be a talented weaver.

Permacultural eclecticism and the commitment to making strong connections between multiple different systems are reflected in the activist

LA Ecovillage

soul of LAEV. The economic and social commitments of this group are evident everywhere, perhaps most keenly in the affordability of housing in the ecovillage. Beyond offering housing at low rates, LAEV is committed to creating sustainable affordability. The sustainability formula allows people to afford their housing over time thereby allowing them to not only age in place, but adapt to life's various financial challenges.

Elsewhere, we see the way in which villagers bring environmentalism to social justice initiatives or social justice concerns to environmental issues. In many ways, LAEV is a cluster of activism where sustainability happens. It is a place that facilitates human connection around sustainability. Ron Milam described this buzz of activity.

Fig. 3.7: *Making seed balls at a permaculture workshop.*

I remember one day it was a Sunday like this, and I walked in and upstairs the bicycle kitchen was having a meeting with their core membership; in the lobby the food co-op was distributing food and out in the garden was Cultivating Sustainable Communities which has an office right there. They were having a board meeting, and then I think there was a school group touring.

Community Outreach and Connection

Fig. 3.8: *Neighboring.*

Ecovillages everywhere struggle with insularity. Choosing to live in a radically different way from dominant society means that those in your immediate vicinity are liable to think you are a bit nuts. And, in order to redirect the course of daily life by acting in ways counter to dominant society, participating in the immediate community beyond the ecovillage can be challenging.

LA Ecovillage

In speaking with LA Ecovillagers it was clear that many recognize the risks of insularity and endeavor to connect with their immediate neighbors. As a concept, LAEV extends beyond the confines of the buildings which house intentional community members, and the intention of bringing surrounding neighbors into LAEV is strong. Events are open to the public, workshops regularly target school children as well as adults and there is a distinct sense of openness to the larger neighborhood. There may not be as much uptake of that openness as some LAEV would like, but that too is an issue being pursued.

Esfandiar was one of the founding members of LAEV, but moved back to his native Iran in 1994 when he realized that much of what he was learning about sustainable practice was a return to earlier, pre-industrial ways of doing things. He thought he could learn more in Iran. He and his wife spent time in small farming communities where traditional ways of life persisted. A problem however was migration out of these communities. Esfandiar and his wife hoped to find out what the problems were that propelled people away and how to bring them back. Working with the communities, they addressed many problems, but people were still leaving. After years of working together they hit upon the root problem: a concept of *progress* that was all about leaving the village, going to Tehran or other cities where the promises of progress could be found. It was this idea, this psychological sense that old ways are not as good as new ways, that instigated the move to the cities and away from traditional, sustainable living.

Now back at LAEV, Esfandiar's goal is to help redefine what constitutes *progress*. He wants to participate in a movement of creating alternative models for progress and said that "Here in LA, where Hollywood churns out an idea of progress as consumerism, maybe we can create a counter to that and redirect some of that attention."

As Esfandiar described it, this is both the challenge and the possibility of forging closer ties with LAEV's immediate neighbors. "Many of the people on this street are immigrants who came here to pursue that dream of progress. To them, planting a fruit tree in the middle of the street may not seem like progress as much as getting a new car." For Esfandiar and others, playing a role in shifting the parameters for what

LA Ecovillage

Fig. 3.9: *Traffic Calming Tea.*

constitutes *making it* is a significant way that they can make a difference
in their immediate neighborhood as well as more broadly.

While there seems to be a certain amount of anxiety on the part of
LA ecovillagers as to how well they are connecting to their neighbors,
the inclusiveness of LAEV seems uniquely evident. The tour of LAEV
that is given on a regular basis includes the whole neighborhood. There
is no distinction in the way LAEV is presented between outside and inside
the community: the buildings down the street, the park and the trees on
the street corners are all included in the presentation of LAEV. Indeed,
Lois Arkin described LAEV as including 500 people who live in the two
blocks, most of whom may not know they live in an ecovillage, but have
a consciousness that something is going on.

Each Sunday LAEV holds a community potluck, and on the warm
July night of our visit, the potluck happened in the street — literally.
Tables were brought out and placed in the street, benches and chairs circled the table and everyone brought their food, plates and utensils and sat
down. We could have eaten in the backyard, but eating in the street

means enacting multiple LAEV goals simultaneously: creating community with the shared meal, retraining cars and offering up small ongoing resistances to car culture by planting ourselves in the street and being a part of the neighborhood. In the backyard privacy and insularity would be ensured. Here, LA Ecovillagers open themselves up to the involvement of their neighborhood in whatever form that might take.

That night in addition to the many strange and/or delighted looks from passersby, surprise took the form of three improbable guests. Loud and overbearing, Ron parked his SUV in front of us, and he and his two intimidating companions approached the table. With some hostility and clearly expecting to be turned away, the entourage asked to join us. The asking was more of a dare, an opportunity to prove us hypocrites in our well-intentioned community meal. But instead of turning these people away, more chairs were brought out, plates and bowls and utensils found, and the community expanded its circle to include three more.

Cultivating Action

LA Ecovillage is very much a cultivator of activism — whether by fighting environmental injustice, launching a local food garden or creating a bike shop. We found that LAEV's commitment to social justice at the local level of one city neighborhood has broad impacts beyond the daily lives of the members of this community. By networking with the larger neighborhood and its residents, organizing bike kitchens and planting trees, LAEV spreads its effects from the local outward. While projects have lived and died, one can only imagine how many minds have been changed along the way and will continue changing. In 2007, Lois Arkin attended the Ecovillage Network of the Americas Council meeting. It was held in the Atlantic Rainforest in Brazil. She described looking out over miles and miles of rainforest — rainforest that is being bulldozed at a rate of one football field per second to support contemporary habits and lifestyles. Feeling the awe and weight of all that forest Lois described thinking, "This is why I do what I do. If we don't change how we live in cities, there's no hope for the lungs of the planet."

Greening Grey

ONE OF THE ÉNDURING REALITIES of 21st-century North America is that we are increasingly a population of older people. In 1900, 4% of the US population was over the age of 65. By 2015, about 15% of the population of North America will be over the age 65. And by 2050, it's expected that 20% of the population will be over the age of 65, with 1/10 over the age of 80.[1] Among other things, this demographic shift has heralded an urgent need to create new, or nourish existing, appropriate and meaningful support systems for later life, including affordable, comfortable housing.

The first large-scale *active-adult* community — Sun City, Arizona — was created in 1960 by Del Webb. Its creation signaled recognition that a large swath of the population was aging, no longer a part of the paid workforce, yet still active and residing independently. Since then, retirement communities have popped up throughout North America, with some areas of Canada and the US populated almost entirely by folks over the age of 75.

At the same time that built environments have arisen to meet the needs of active middle- to upper-class seniors, a more pressing and less well-addressed need exists for poor seniors, for those who are infirm or frail and for the large number of increasingly isolated old folks in urban centers, suburban and rural outposts. Assisted living, nursing and long-term care facilities now exist to address physical needs for mostly those who can afford them or who have sufficient insurance. While meeting physical needs, these facilities do not as often include the kind of community and social connectivity necessary for good health at any age. And, when older persons continue to live independently and age in place, the environments they find themselves in are often not able to meet their changing needs. In either case, a common result is increasing isolation and loneliness in later life — two factors which are consequential for both physical and mental health.

During the 1995 heat wave in Chicago, Illinois for example, 700 people died directly or indirectly as a result of the heat. Seniors were especially vulnerable, perishing in unexpectedly high numbers not because they were frail or in poor health —at least not entirely — but because they were socially isolated.[2] Eric Klinenberg, in his compelling analysis of the disaster, described the way that hundreds died alone behind locked doors and sealed windows. The social and the built environment converged in Chicago with a disastrous result: as older people were isolated in homes with limited air circulation, their chances of poor health effects increased. Epidemiological data examining the Chicago heat wave and the one in Paris a few years later found that people without or with limited proximal social ties died at disproportionate rates. Anything that facilitated social contact such as membership in a club or owning a pet was associated with a decreased risk of death.

In general, seniors who have active social networks tend to have better health and greater longevity than those who are isolated. While not all seniors who live alone are isolated or lonely, those who live alone are more likely than those who live with others to be emotionally depressed, physically isolated, economically impoverished and fearful of crime. Some of the factors that increase risks associated with isolation and limited support systems include being poor and living in a deteriorating neighborhood.

Aging in place is a concept that has newly become popular in thinking about senior housing: providing the kinds of living situations that enable people to live at home longer — to age in place — has become a goal in many home designs. Building spaces that can adapt to people's changing bodily abilities and situations is desirable.

Yet, aging in place is not problem-free. One concern comes when the place within which one lives undergoes profound changes and may no longer resemble the familiar *home* and community it once was. Klinenberg notes that aging in place often means outliving social contacts, no longer being a part of work or other familiar groups. Friends, relatives, children or others move away, and neighborhoods change demographically, leaving those that remain in unfamiliar and sometimes uncomfortable contexts. People's environments change while they stay where they are, making strange what was once familiar. Consequently, people may be living in individual residences that are appropriate to their changing needs, but their larger community may not be. It may not provide local services, shops, gathering places, fresh air or opportunities for exercise. Or, even if it does provide those things, individuals may not know to take advantage of them if surroundings have changed and become unfamiliar.

What all of this highlights is that aging in place is not enough — *aging in community* is required. As a result, and in response to some of the social issues inherent with aging populations, there have been various approaches to affordable senior housing as well as intentional communities targeting aging people. As we mentioned in Chapter 2, the idea of elder cohousing has taken firm hold in North America. What these and other innovative approaches to housing in later life emphasize is the desirability of aging in community, rather than just aging in place as individuals. Aging in community may enhance social connectivity and enrich lives. Many are hoping this is true, and across North America niche markets for aging populations are emerging from top-down developers and grass-roots movements alike. Every day we find new instances of groups starting organized and ad-hoc residential communities for their own and other's anticipated aging needs.

The linking of green building design with these housing endeavors is a newer phenomenon, however. Green communities for older folks tackle serious issues in the aging community. In particular, building green can mitigate some of the financial risks associated with aging. Typically, people become less economically secure later in life. As we leave the workforce, we rely on fixed incomes to meet our needs and often take on increased health care costs; our financial well-being diminishes. Heating

Laura Mamo

Fig. 4.1: *Chez Soi from Cavendish Avenue.*

and cooling one's home, for example, have been cited as burdensome for many older people. In cold and hot climates, such difficulty can lead to serious health consequences. But building green can help: by providing environmentally sustainable alternatives, the economic burden of heating and cooling can be lessened.

Similarly, building green can also enhance health — an issue of concern for everybody, but particularly for an older population, many of whom may be living with various chronic conditions. The improved indoor air quality of green buildings, the lack of toxic off-gassing in building materials and the health benefits of visual and physical access to green spaces are all important factors making green elder housing a logical combination.

One such effort to merge the goals of green building and aging in community can be found in the diverse neighborhood of Notre-Dame-de-Grâce in the city of Montréal. There, on a busy corner in a neighborhood close to downtown, with a history of housing immigrants and the poor, is the newly developed Chez Soi — part of an ongoing redevelopment known as Benny Farm.

Social Housing: Historical Roots, Current Visions

A history of social housing can be read in the foundations of Benny Farm. Benny Farm gets its name from Walter Benny, a Scottish manufacturer who bought land on the island of Montréal in 1838. The property was farmed by his descendents until 1944, and a residential development was built there in 1946. In 1947 the newly established Central Mortgage and Housing Corporation (CMHC) took the development over to provide housing for returning World War II veterans. Benny Farm was one of the first government-subsidized housing developments in Canada.

Drawing on the concept of a *garden city*, the buildings were arranged into u-shapes, creating common courtyards where children could play and people could gather. While the building and landscape design affected the daily lives of the residents, it was the people who really made Benny Farm into a strong and cohesive community. The veterans, diverse in ethnic, cultural and geographical backgrounds, were deeply connected by their shared experience of the war and their renewed sense of building family in prosperous North America. As a result, demographically, the vast majority living at Benny Farm were young families. Hundreds and hundreds of children were born and grew up together during the 1950s and 1960s at Benny Farm. To this day, chat groups on the Internet crop up so old Benny Farmers can reconnect and share fond memories. That it was a tight-knit and vibrant place to live was amply evident in the outward manifestations of thriving community organizations, sports teams and a local newsletter.

Things began to change, however, in the 1980s. As the population grew older, adult children moved away, parents aged and many long-time residents relocated, moved to care facilities or passed away. The buildings fell into disrepair and became burdensome and problematic for the remaining, mostly elderly, population. Benny Farm became an example of many of the social problems Klinenberg described with aging in place: a previously vibrant, tight-knit community gradually became a deteriorating neighborhood as folks moved out or moved on and those that remained became not only frail but isolated.

In 1989, the CMHC announced plans to demolish the old Benny Farm buildings and to privatize a large percentage of the buildings and land. This ignited an immediate response of outrage among remaining residents and community activists, who, while aware of problems with the buildings, believed they could be renovated and restored if resources were allocated to do so. Community members began an engagement with plans for redeveloping Benny Farm that, in certain sectors, is still underway today. Throughout the 1990s, many plans were put forward and disregarded, yet community involvement remained strong. Finally in 2002, the Canada Lands Corporation (CLC to whom the CMHC sold its contract for Benny Farm in 1999) agreed to formal, public consultation, and the Benny Farm Task Force was formed to ensure that the needs of the people were heard.

The task force wanted the history of Benny Farm to be preserved — both in terms of the buildings themselves as well as community spirit and a commitment to affordability. In fact, they believed doing so would be central to the creation of a vibrant and sustainable community. These recommendations were taken into consideration in the ultimate plan for redevelopment which was approved in 2002. The plan called for a 35-40% renovation of existing structures combined with new construction. It maintained a focus on low-cost housing and commitment to green spaces. The spirit of social housing would remain intact at Benny Farm.

Chez Soi at Green Energy Benny Farm

Passion radiates off of Daniel Pearl as he describes the ideas, accomplishments and future plans for Benny Farm. Danny is an architect with L'OEUF (L'Office de L'Eclectisme Urbain et Fonctionnel), the firm whose vision helped develop and build the innovative, Holcim award-winning project that exists today at Benny Farm.

We met with Danny on a summer's day in one of the comfortable gathering spaces on the ground floor of Chez Soi. He had just finished giving us a tour of the site; his excitement at what exists and what is still in process was evident with his every gesture, wide, smiling face and enthusiastic, booming voice. He and his partners are deeply passionate and committed to making Benny Farm not only an innovative, sustainable housing design, but also a model of social housing for the 21st century.

To hear Danny speak about the project, two things are immanently clear: first, that this was a long and sometimes frustrating struggle, propelled forward by deep commitment to the ideals that undergird it and second, that the entire project is a collaborative endeavor, manifested through the efforts of many, including volunteers who like Danny share passion for their cause.

Danny and his co-founding business partner, Mark Poddubiuk, began their involvement with the redevelopment of Benny Farm in the early 1990s. Upon moving to the Notre-Dame-de-Grâce (NDG) neighborhood, Mark became involved with the NDG Community Council's housing committee, the group most intimately engaged in challenging the demolition and privatization of the Benny Farm site. In 1992, the architects embarked on a study of Benny Farm as it existed then and as it could potentially be transformed in the future.

Among other things, their study was a critique of the CMHC redevelopment plans to demolish and privatize. From their perspective, the deterioration was superficial, requiring the kind of overhaul that could be expected after 40 or 50 years. The more important elements of the buildings — their design and character (natural daylight in every room including kitchens and bathroom, cross ventilation in every unit were in fact better than what is typically designed and built today. Further, as years of vibrancy and community activism highlighted, the social character of the complex was always healthy.

Ultimately, Danny and Mark wanted all of these elements to be taken into consideration in the question of what to do with Benny Farm — and what emerged was a vision for a sustainable community. As Danny described it, "the opportunity latent in decline and failure — renovation — is an important element in a global and long-range concept of sustainability." Their stance against wholesale demolition was as much about listening to community wants and needs as it was about adhering to an ethic of environmentalism. For Danny and Mark, these things are inextricably interconnected. From the start they were operating within a definition of sustainability that inherently includes community rights.

As part of their study, Mark and Danny visited the Netherlands where they saw 70 projects in 8 days and were struck by the notion of the

European land trust model that housing is a right, not a commodity. Building on some of these ideas and others, l'OEUF and the NDG Community Council's Housing Committee sought to create a vision for Benny Farm that incorporated socio-cultural values into its mission. Many studies, consultations, negotiations and setbacks later, the plan for redevelopment that was approved in 2002 included a pilot of what the original vision had been. The pilot included three properties, of the much larger overall redevelopment, which would encompass the social and environmental goals fermenting since the early 1990s. These three properties would be overseen by Énergie Verte Benny Farm (EVBF or Green Energy Benny Farm) which was established for that purpose through a $3-million Federation of Canadian Municipalities grant. EVBF is a non-profit, community-owned energy services company that produces, provides and promotes renewable energy and green buildings.

The three projects initially set to fall under the EVBF umbrella were (1) Chez Soi, non-profit affordable rental housing for seniors (the focus of this chapter), (2) Project Z.O.O. (Zone of Opportunity), a not-for-profit housing cooperative created in the fall of 2000 to meet the rising need in

Daphne Ferguson

Fig. 4.2: *Green Energy Benny Farm Solar Panels.*

Montréal for adequate, affordable housing for families and (3) HCNDG, affordable home ownership for middle-income residents. Currently, the first two are still a part of EVBF, and Chez Soi has been the most integrated into green technologies. Chez Soi and Z.O.O. share physical, social and economic infrastructure and, together, provide for an intergenerational green community.

Chez Soi is a non-profit, flexible support senior's housing complex with 91 apartments. It was designed to attain a LEED gold rating, and the hope is that the green energy services ensure that Chez Soi's energy bills are buffered from rising prices for seniors on fixed incomes. Some of the green features of Chez Soi include hybrid solar and geothermal recharge and a solar wall. It is designed to receive a green roof, return stormwater into percolation beds and recycle greywater for filling toilets. Each unit includes radiant floor geothermal heating. In addition, Green Energy Benny Farm used local knowledge and resources, and many building materials were salvaged from the older buildings (bricks and radiators were reused in the new construction of 16 units at neighboring Z.O.O.). Joining these innovative building technologies with a commitment to aging in place is not only an indication of a commitment to social, economic and environmental welfare, but it also represents an increasingly available and important strategy.

Chez Soi is the kind of community that enhances social well-being. The building includes several common spaces in addition to the individual apartments in which residents live. Inside there are meeting rooms with glassed-in walls providing ample light and a large dining room which is surrounded by full-length windows looking out onto the street. The dining room contains tables and chairs and is almost always in use by somebody. Outside, community gardens and pedestrian walkways connect Chez Soi with the other planned and existing buildings of Benny Farm. This is where the multi-generational quality comes to life. While Chez Soi itself is a senior residence, families, young adults, teenagers and small children share the outside spaces as residents of adjacent buildings, making Chez Soi part of a much more intergenerational community.

Benny Farm itself is situated in close proximity to multiple services and amenities. From Chez Soi it is less than a block to bus lines, a large

Fig. 4.3: *Green Energy Benny Farm Community Garden.*

Laura Mamo

grocery store and pharmacy and a long city block of restaurants and services. Health care facilities and social services are also a block away. In addition to the ample green space surrounding Chez Soi itself, a public park with a swimming pool is nearby. All that the larger city of Montréal has to offer is a bus ride away. The long history of community activism around the site has ensured that local interests, culture and heritage are integrated into the redevelopment of Benny Farm.

Living Green at Chez Soi

It was early evening, but the sky was dark outside. It was a cold mid-January night. Outside the full-length windows that encase two sides of the Chez Soi common room, snow fell in a steady white curtain. Yet it felt warm and hospitable inside: music was playing, food was being served and about 40 people sat companionably around the four-top tables scattered throughout the room. Some brought in more chairs to join their friends, a line of people sat against the window and several stood around the food table, chatting. Friends asked friends to "save their seats" as they got up for food at the long counter in the back. Some got plates of food

Fig. 4.4:
Daphne Ferguson
Conducting
Sustainability Workshop
with Chez Soi Residents.

for their less mobile friends and table-mates. There wasn't an empty table here. Nobody sat alone or removed from others.

Everything was oriented toward the front of the room where a large screen had been erected with projected images displaying various stages of Chez Soi's construction. Most of the folks chatting, eating and talking together were women, mostly over 70. In the front of the room, a group of young 20- to 30-somethings sat and talked, periodically greeting newcomers to the room. These young people were the organizers of the night's event.

The gathering was the first of its kind at Chez Soi: a sustainability presentation, emceed by the newly hired operating officer, Daphne. Among the other presenters gathered at the front were members of the EVBF technical and managerial team. One of these young men joked that he was parked nearby if he had to make a quick escape. The others laughed, masking a common anxiety shared among the gathered group: anxiety stemming from problems with the heating and other systems that had plagued Benny Farm over the past year. We were told it had not been an easy path to a fully occupied and working Chez Soi. The project met with some serious problems through its first winter, and that day's

meeting was organized to provide residents the opportunity to understand more deeply the kinds of technologies that power and heat their
lives and to learn what they themselves can do to improve functioning.

Despite this history, a spirit of good will seemed to permeate the
crowd; they did not appear anxious or angry, as the representatives of
EVBF seemed to fear. The residents socialized, ate and sat patiently ready
to listen, to learn and to find out more about the green design and engineering features of their building. Alex Hill, operations manager of
EVBF, began by outlining the green infrastructure of Chez Soi. Bob
Butler, president of the board of directors of EVBF described the geothermal system and greywater recovery systems. Bob's style was friendly
and casual, and he explained all of these technologies in plain language,
making the complex systems seem straightforward. There were lots of
questions for him — especially regarding the concept of greywater and
what it means for water quality — and Bob answered them all.

After the presentations were completed and the questions answered,
the evening shifted gears. While the first part of the program was meant
to transfer knowledge from the builders and operators to the residents
about the innovative green technologies that infuse their homes, the second part was meant to be interactive and draw on the ideas and expertise
of residents as well. Kathleen Usher, a member of the board of EVBF, got
up to address the crowd. First, she initiated a brainstorming session on the
very idea of community. Residents called out terms they associated with
this abstract concept: friendliness, cooperation, consideration, Chez Soi,
gossip, home, church, people, unity, love, understanding, harmony,
respect, communication, enjoyment, congregation, security, good health,
comfortable. One woman broke into song as her contribution to what
community meant to her. The next concept for brainstorming was sustainability. When asked what sustainable community meant, some of the
answers included: meets basic needs, is equitable, enhances physical,
social and mental well-being, promotes mutual support and is democratic
and empowering.

It was with the next question that the wealth of knowledge in the
room truly became apparent: what can you personally do to promote sustainability? One very old woman in a green sweatshirt and thick glasses

began a long line of ideas about how to live green. As she spoke about gardening, composting, hanging clothes to dry, reusing containers, wasting nothing and a litany of other things it became clear that her generation was raised on sustainability. These practices were natural in a pre-disposable, pre-plastic era. Against the backdrop of the great depression, they were a means of survival rather than an ideology. The ordinary daily practices of older generations are increasingly seen as extraordinary efforts in today's landscape. It is only recently that the concept of disposable has come to dominate, that the things we buy come in many layers of packaging and furthermore, that buying has gone from an occasional practice to a full-fledged hobby for some.

In listening to the residents at Chez Soi, it was obvious that while green innovations in building and design have much to offer an aging population in terms of community, healthy buildings and flexible, accessible spaces, the green building movement can also draw from the valuable resource that is the collective knowledge of those who spent their formative years living green before there were more wasteful alternatives. In fact, those with the most knowledge and expertise about ways to live green may just be members of our aging population.

Fig. 4.5: *Chez Soi Community Bulletin Board.*

Sustainable Aging in Community

Whatever heating-system issues residents dealt with in their first winter, one thing that seemed absolutely certain is that Chez Soi is a great place to live. Walking along busy Cavendish Avenue on any given evening, you might look into the huge windows of Chez Soi and see 30 or 40 people gathering for a meal. If it is a Friday night, you might see them gathered around a screen to watch a film. On a Monday or Thursday you might see groups gathered around various tables playing cards, boggle or backgammon. And on any warm day you could wander to the gardens and open spaces and find people sitting on benches reading, talking or relaxing.

Laura Lee Reid is one of those residents who loves living at Chez Soi. She described the meaning she derives from helping the residents, most of whom are significantly older than she is. She also describes how, when she recently hurt her back, people came knocking on her door with offers to help her. When asked what makes the building special, she replied

> The dining room. Without it, we'd just be tenants
> in a building. With the dining room, we're a com-
> munity. It's a place where we can congregate, learn
> each other's names and hear each other's stories.

To hear Laura speak of it and to watch the interactions that make Chez Soi a vibrant place, it is evident that the visions of social housing which enrich, enliven and improve people's lives are manifest in this corner of Benny Farm. Here, social sustainability is illuminated, and aging in community is in progress.

The idea of aging in community is part of a broader social housing movement. It is clear that as bodies and minds age and lifestyles change that people have different needs as well as desires. Allowing people not only to stay in place, but to stay in a vibrant expansive place with social interaction, intergenerational contacts as well as easy access to health care, transportation and services such as grocery outlets is increasingly understood as not only desirable, but also sustainable for healthy aging. In cities and towns across North America, senior housing developments are increasingly supported with tax incentives and demanded by taxpayers. In Florida, for example, 73 towns, cities and counties are participating in a community initiative, Communities for a Lifetime, aimed at strengthening relationships between local aging organizations and community partners. The goal is improved housing, transportation, health care and efficient use of natural resources with the outcome of creating opportunities that encourage a high quality of life and independence for older

Fig. 4.6: *Chez Soi.*

adults.³ In San Francisco, BRIDGE Housing Corporation, a leader in affordable housing design, is developing green senior housing in high-density neighborhoods and in association with major aging organizations.

The developers, managers and residents of Chez Soi understand that aging in community is not only healthier for the people residing there, but also healthy for the environment. Chez Soi makes use of the benefits that high density offers: access to resources and transportation necessary to live car-free and independently. The other projects that make up Green Energy Benny Farm (e.g., Z.O.O., the affordable housing project for families) make for an intergenerational community, which pays off in terms of health and happiness, but also in terms of resource-use. A mixed-age population makes mixed use of the neighborhood at differing hours.

It is such partnerships and commitments that we think will allow the built environment and the organic texture of neighborhoods to come together to enhance the future for aging in community. Including innovative engineering and architectural design features into building and renovation plans is a testament to the flexibility and forward thinking of those who have worked on this project. The built-in green features will aid in promoting the kind of economic and environmental sustainability envisioned by the interdisciplinary team that made Chez Soi a reality. The residents at Benny Farm exemplify the ways the social commitments of a few insiders can generate the changes and perseverance needed to create sustainable communities. Likewise, as the older women of Benny Farm showed us, it may just be the lessons of conservation from generations in concert with the tools of the day that will best enhance today's needs for economic, social and environmental sustainability.

Affordable Green Housing

IT WAS A SATURDAY IN JANUARY, the rainy season in the bay area of San Francisco, but this day was sunny and warm with a cool breeze from ocean fog. Kevin Edelbrock, the Property Supervisor of Folsom/Dore, an award-winning green affordable housing project, met us at the apartments where he had arranged for us to talk with some residents. We assembled in the large, open room on the side of the building.

Love came in with his large dog. He was a young man who reminded us of a skateboard kid — a bit messy with a mumbling voice. He made little eye contact, and while ultimately very open he was initially hesitant to share with us. He told us he hadn't had a stable place to live in a long time, that he was just starting to "get his life together." Love had been homeless for several years before being referred to Folsom/Dore. He said "I didn't think that I would find a home for myself and my dog." Once he warmed up and we discussed the neighborhood, weather and his dog's favorite walking spots, he spoke surprisingly clearly about the importance of Folsom/Dore in his life

> When I moved here I continued to destroy myself
> for several months, I was hanging out with people
> who damaged me physically and in my mind, and
> I was taking chemicals that threw my mind out of

balance. I let all of that go. I am happy waking up
and walking my dog, saying hi to people, my neighbors, whoever happens to be around. I enjoy myself
again, my home, the changing weather. I'm at a
good place ... I never knew I would be so lucky.

Love, it turned out, was similar to many other residents at Folsom/
Dore. His health was severely compromised from many years of living on
and off the streets and on and off drugs. For Love, like many others,
Folsom/Dore would also be his last home. He died a few months after
our meeting. His death, unlike many others, was a shock for the staff and
residents. He was relatively young and was stabilizing his life. Years of
drug abuse, however, had compromised his liver and kidneys, and on the
weekend of his death alcohol shut his system down completely. He died
on the living room sofa in his apartment.

Before Love's death he talked to one of the support staff about his sense
that his time might be coming. He told her he felt more relaxed than he
had in a long time, and it made him a little worried. "People say once you
get rid of it [the adrenalin of living on the streets] your body allows itself
to let in the sickness." The support services staff organized a memorial
service for Love with the assistance of his mother, and people from all
over turned out to remember him.

Vernon, a Vietnam vet, was another Folsom/Dore resident who seemed
to be in a good place in his life. He had also been homeless for several
years before coming to Folsom/Dore, and when we talked, his big news
was a recent reconnection with his sister in Oakland and that he was
"finally off drugs" for good. He explained

When my Case Manager asked me why I wanted
housing I told her that I wanted a place to look at
all of my stuff one more time, I wanted a place to
invite my family so we could speak again and I
wanted a place to wake up happy in so that I could
let go. My health isn't so good, it's positive for me
to think that way. I still drive, but I know I won't

be driving for long. I know a little about what to expect.

Vernon continued to tell us he liked his life at Folsom/Dore. He liked having a bed and a place to call home. He mostly talked with the maintenance man and the night manager. "They make my day — we get along," he told us. "If I had known how good life could feel I would have taken better care of myself before." Like Love, many years of drugs and street life left Vernon's body and health severely compromised, and not long after our interview with him, the Folsom/Dore staff members were organizing a memorial service for him.

This is life and death at the Folsom/Dore apartments in the South of Market area of San Francisco. As Nina, the Placement Coordinator described it, it is often the "last safe, clean, comfortable" place many formerly homeless men and women spend their days.

The Context: The City of San Francisco

San Francisco is a city of stark contradictions: a tourist destination and blue-collar industrial center; a working immigration magnet and a high-tech Visa 1 hub; home to some of the most beautiful landscapes in the world, yet a city littered with crumbling infrastructures resembling other distressed major cities; a population with large numbers of newly rich entrepreneurs living alongside an even larger number of homeless and working-poor residents. Given its beauty, high-tech and entrepreneurial spirit it is not surprising that San Francisco is also home to a burgeoning architectural and green building movement where design, technology and progressive values merge to produce new and innovative built environments. It did not take long for innovations in building to meet the social needs of urban environments.

Within this nexus of contradictions and social entrepreneurialism, myriad small-scale solutions have emerged to address the social needs of the city. One of the most pressing social needs of San Francisco is that a large percentage of people live on the streets.[1] A recent solution proposed for this problem by the Mayor's Office on Housing is *supportive housing*, an effort to move homeless persons directly from the streets to permanent apartments with an added layer of on-site social service support to aid their transition to independence and successful residential living. For those formerly homeless men and women living without severe mental health problems, this approach has been heralded by many as a promising solution to chronic homelessness.

The Folsom/Dore Apartments, situated at the entrance to the South of Market (SOMA) neighborhood at the corner of Folsom Street and Dore Alley, was the first mixed-supportive housing apartment complex to open in San Francisco with 40 of 98 units set aside for formerly homeless individuals. The first residents moved into Folsom/Dore on March 30, 2005. Folsom/Dore is an experiment at the intersection of social justice and environmental design. When Mayor Gavin Newsom cut the ribbon at the building's grand opening ceremony on April 20, 2005, the event was attended by a large audience of people from non-profit housing, social service organizations, local community groups and neighborhood establishments. Many had participated directly in the interdisciplinary teams needed to bring the vision of Folsom/Dore to reality. In his address to the crowd, the mayor said

> Today we stand at the entrance to the Folsom Dore Apartments — a permanent exit to chronic homelessness. Folsom Dore is a showcase of the City's commitment to provide 1500 newly constructed, HDC-owned, supportive housing units for the chronically homeless. Citizens Housing Corporation has created a best practice in San Francisco.[2]

Folsom/Dore was also a winner of the National Green Building Award from the National Institute of Architects and the 2007 Award of Excellence for Affordable Housing Built Responsibly from the Home Depot Foundation. It is certified LEED Silver. The building is owned and managed by Citizens Housing Corporation, a non-profit housing developer. On-site services with the goal of continuous, ongoing support to maintain life stability are provided to residents by Lutheran Social Services of Northern California, a private non-profit agency.

Driving down Folsom Street with its contradictory mix of old and new, decay and gentrification, Folsom/Dore is an unmistakable presence as bamboo open-air balconies rise on the horizon. Its five stories occupy most of one square block, and every detail of its structure has been carefully designed. Along Folsom Street a large window front abuts the street, blending nicely with the adjacent commercial corridor. Over this rises a slightly set-back, mostly stucco exterior building with external wooden balconies. Along the side street, Dore Alley, lies the entrance encircled by bamboo plantings with exterior breezeways and stairwells visible overhead. Designed using bold colors and seamless indoor and outdoor spaces, Folsom/Dore creates a transition from the urban energy of the neighborhood to the private and semi-private spaces inside.

Folsom/Dore is not only an experiment in reducing chronic homelessness, but it is also an experiment in mixed-income residential housing. Residents range from fully employed high-tech workers to people living

Fig. 5.1: Folsom/Dore Apartment Building.

on disability. Twenty units are set aside for the chronically homeless (i.e. direct from homeless individuals) and another 20 units are set aside for individuals and families coming from homelessness or at risk of homelessness. Households with Section 8 Vouchers and other subsidies are welcome, and there are several affordable housing units rented at 60% of San Francisco's average median income. Current residents include individuals with HIV/AIDS, developmentally disabled adults, welfare-to-work participants and individuals with mental illness and other disabilities including substance abuse. There are also market-rate units thrown into this mix.

Fig. 5.2: Intersection of Folsom Street and Dore Alley.

Brian Rose

SOMA:
The Neighborhood and Its History

One of the first rules of setting up an ecovillage is to pay attention to the land — the site — upon which you are building. Whether for the spiritual taboo of building on a First Nation's burial ground, the ecological fallout from building on a fragile habitat or the political backlash of building on land steeped in controversy, place matters. Architects and developers also know this rule well. There are intriguing, intertwined histories that underlie Folsom/Dore's foundations.

Folsom/Dore gets its name from its cross streets: it sits at the intersection of Folsom Street and Dore Alley in the heart of the neighborhood referred to as South of Market (SOMA). This designation contrasts with more polished and tourist neighborhoods North of Market Street. As described by Kathleen Connell and Paul Gabriel, SOMA emerged as a somewhat typical port neighborhood: a center of commerce with cargo entering from and redirected to destinations all over the country and globe. Populated by working immigrants — largely Filipino longshoremen and merchant marines — the SOMA neighborhood has historically been a low-rent area with multiple single-room occupancy hotels. It is connected by rail lines to the naval yard at Hunter's Point; it lies above the Embarcadero port where servicepeople arrived for temporary leave and, to the north, it adjoins the Tenderloin, a historically gritty area filled with massage and sex parlors, streetwalkers and gambling establishments.

As a low-rent district throughout most of the twentieth century, SOMA attracted new immigrants, working artists, merchant marines and other sea-faring workers. SOMA also became home (especially in the area of South Park) to many African American families who were denied housing north of Folsom Street, San Francisco's 20th-century color line.

Given the mix of people living in this neighborhood, an undercurrent of progressive ideas and political activism was present. In 1934, Harry Bridges led a great strike, successfully shutting down the port and eventually the whole city — an event which led to a series of dock worker rights. Around the 1960s, South of Market began to attract a burgeoning gay male leather community, and for the next two decades leather bars and bath houses sprang up throughout the neighborhood. A leather economy took form in the 1960s with several leather bars occupying a three-block strip along Folsom Street.[3] The sexual openness and political threads of SOMA were carried forward into the 70s by both a confident post-Stonewall, pre-AIDS gay population and a diverse set of politically engaged groups and organizations. Together, these gave birth to various neighborhood-based organizations and what evolved into a history of coalition activist organizations at the forefront of worker, people of color, youth, immigrant, sexual, elderly and other radical-progressive political work, including non-profit community housing developers dedicated to affordable housing for those in need.

In the 1980s, the vibrant community of South of Market was devastated by the AIDS epidemic, and the city's somewhat panicked response to this health concern was to close the bath houses and sex clubs that had been the economic life blood of the SOMA neighborhood. In response, the neighborhood with its histories of activism organized two leather events:

the Folsom Street Fair and Dore Alley (or "Up Your Alley") in 1984 and 1985 respectively, to raise money and awareness in an atmosphere of playfulness and celebration and to demonstrate to the world that South of Market continued as a vital and vibrant part of the city. Today, the Folsom Street Fair attracts hundreds of thousands of people, and both events have kept the neighborhood and its queer leather community alive.[4]

During the late 1990s, SOMA exploded again — this time as a center of the dot-com technology boom with its adjoining Media Gulch to the southeast. Located at the entrances to the freeways that feed into the heart of the Silicon Valley but offering large spaces at relatively cheap rent and a much hipper address, South of Market became a hot bed of internet and biotech start-ups. As some of these start-ups converted into big money, South of Market became awash in the trimmings of new wealth: restaurants, martini bars, design and architectural firms, yoga studios, fancy hotels, a plethora of newly constructed live-work lofts and a new ballpark with restaurants and bars to support incoming crowds.

As the high-tech bubble burst, South of Market felt the effect: buildings stood vacant, and incomplete building projects were abandoned. Yet much of the gentrification remained, and new projects continued. This, in part, is thanks to the new major league ballpark, a new conference center, world class museums, the renovation and expansion of the Westfield Mall on Market and Mission streets, a vibrant organic food market and the biotech campus of a leading research University, UCSF. This gentrification has fundamentally changed the area, but has not fully eclipsed the history and feel of the neighborhood that remains in several pockets throughout a large stretch of avenues and streets.

South of Market remains a place where new immigrants settle (St. Patrick's church, across from Yerba Buena Gardens, a great symbol of the gentrification of South of Market, still celebrates its masses in Tagalog); the leather scene and a scattering of gay bars remain a palpable presence and, while the soaring rents of the 1990s pushed out many residents, alternative clubs and art galleries, many such venues remain. SOMA, for good and bad, also continues to be a neighborhood providing low-rents, single room hotels, drug recovery programs and the often concomitant burdens of poverty, homelessness and struggles with drug addiction.

But what better place to plan and build a mixed income housing complex than at the intersection of social and environmental justice? Folsom/Dore's foundations are as complex and multi-layered as the city itself. A diversity of ghosts haunts its grounds maintaining its ties to the neighborhood's legacy: a commitment to social justice, a recognition of its working class and political roots, a celebration of the activism of the queer leather community and an homage to those who have died from the ravages of homelessness, HIV/AIDS or violence. In addition, Folsom/Dore's commitment to style and aesthetics resonates with both the enduring bohemian art culture here as well as the more recent creative energies of the dot-comers.

Fig. 5.3: *Entrance to Folsom/Dore Apartments.*

The Project: Developing Green + Supportive Housing

True to its neighborhood history, Folsom/Dore is the result of a coalition of constituents: the City of San Francisco, David Baker + Partners Architects, Cahill Construction and Citizens Housing Corporation. The Mayor's Office of the City of San Francisco provided $8.8 million in financing, leveraging an additional $18.5 million in state, federal and private funding sources, including state Multifamily Housing Program funds, Federal Home Loan Bank Funds, Citibank credit enhancement and Apollo Housing Capital tax credit equity. Operations are also subsidized through the City's Department of Public Health and HUD's McKinney Act and Section 8 project-based funds.

While a main priority for developing Folsom/Dore was to help end chronic homelessness, an equally important goal was to address the growing environmental problems of our time. The project began in 2001 with

Helen Fitzsimmons

clear guidelines and practices for building green. Daniel Simons, an associate and architect at David Baker + Partners and the project manager of the Folsom/Dore project admitted, "At that time, sustainability was a personal vision of myself and David Baker, but it was not yet part of our institution. We had not yet had a client who wanted to do it." Yet, he continued, "We approach housing from a humanistic standpoint that engenders a sense of community. Those goals don't vary from project to project."

It was their partnership with Citizens Housing that provided the drive to create a truly green project as well as one that met the need for mixed-income supportive housing. Doing so required addressing human and environmental needs side-by-side. Environmentally, Folsom/Dore developed green goals to maximize energy efficiency beyond state minimum standards, to utilize recycled and other materials designed to enhance air quality and reduce off-gassing effects and to minimize residents' reliance on cars for transportation. These building aspects would not only lower economic utility costs for residents, but could potentially improve resident's health through cleaner air and reduced exposure to toxins and through recycling, car share and social services.

In contrast to residents of other communities featured in this book, people who live at Folsom/Dore do not necessarily move to this community with the express purpose of living green. They move here because they need an affordable place to live. Necessity overshadows other considerations. One of the residents admitted to just finding out about the solar energy that very day. In many ways, green living is an accidental consequence of living at Folsom/Dore.

This isn't to say there aren't residents for whom the fact of Folsom/Dore's sustainable design is critical to their experience of living there. There are. "I live in a Green Building," said a woman in a wheelchair when asked what she liked about Folsom/Dore. Another man stated

> Recycling is big here anyway. In this city it is big.
> I have always recycled, always. I mean it is part of
> life. I hear the paint is very good paint. And, what
> else? The solar. I think it is good for me. I'll go live

somewhere else for a week and then come back here
and I'll see and feel the difference ...

We spoke with one young couple who described
explicitly moving to Folsom/Dore for environmental
and social sustainability as well as affordability. They
were drawn by the green mission and were knowl-
edgeable about all the products and design features of
the building. They fell in love with their apartment
— finding it far more clean, spacious and open than
they could previously afford: "... And plus it's just
really cute. It feels like you are going up to your own
tree house. It's just so freaking great, I can't believe
it." It was the green and social goals plus the beauty of the building that
sold these two on moving to Folsom/Dore.

Fig. 5.4: *Folsom/Dore
Resident on Opening Day.*

We toured the building with Kevin Edelbrock, the Property Supervisor
and Nina Berkson, the Placement Coordinator, and they described
Folsom/Dore's green features — some were obvious, others were less so.
Kevin said

The windows are commercial grade, double paned
and are designed to help reduce UV damage to the
apartment and reduce energy consumption. We use
low- to no-VOC paints and sealants which significantly reduce the amount of indoor air pollution and
limit the aggravation of lungs, eyes and even skin that
regular paints can cause. The carpet pads are recycled, thereby saving resources and diverting waste
from landfills. It also reduces our need for cleaning
products as they are easier to clean, more resilient
and tend to last for longer than regular carpets. The
bathroom vinyl flooring consists of 40% recycled
material. Our cabinetry is urea formaldehyde-free
which means the typical glue binding the cabinet
materials together doesn't contain the suspected

human carcinogen urea formaldehyde. Our lighting includes fluorescent and compact fluorescent bulbs.

Folsom/Dore has a solar panel system that supplements the common area electricity. They also have drain-water heat recovery devices that recover hot water from tub drain pipes and are used to preheat cold water which reduces the need to heat additional water.

All of these elements, like those we saw at Benny Farm, have both economic and potential health benefits for residents of Folsom/Dore. Economically, the efficiency of the buildings cuts down on utility expenses for residents. In terms of health, as Kevin's comments above

Fig. 5.5: Breezeway at Folsom/Dore Apartments.

Helen Fitzsimmons

made clear, the use of non-toxic products — from building materials, to paints, to carpets and cleaning supplies — makes a palpable difference in the health of residents. Many of the residents at Folsom/Dore have asthma and other health issues, and the improved indoor air quality achieved through using non-polluting materials helps them.

Further, fresh air is in ample supply at Folsom/Dore. The public environment is smoke-free, and there is access to outside space from all of the apartments as well as built-in breezeway halls on each level. The apartments have fresh-air ventilation as well as access to outside. As Kevin described, "People's apartments here don't have that kind of stagnant smell that a lot have, so especially if residents have health issues, I think that's where the open air vents help with health." In these ways, building green has enhanced public health.

Promoting Social Sustainability at Folsom/Dore

Social sustainability emphasizes human equality, diversity, dignity and respect. Similar to LAEV, Folsom/Dore is an example of environmental justice and brings these social issues to the foreground. The historical legacy of San Francisco and the SOMA neighborhood are represented by residents at Folsom/Dore. Among those we spoke with were a Latina immigrant working mom and her disabled teenage son; a bi-racial black and white gay male couple, one HIV positive and the other negative; a formerly homeless Vietnam vet African American man who was newly living clean and sober and a young bi-racial heterosexual married couple, Asian American and white, who were starting their own high-tech business in their home. Brian, one of the residents at Folsom/Dore, equated the building with the New York City subway, "It's all different walks of life together. From one stop to the next, different people come on." While a shared perspective was not part of every day, each of the residents believed in the building and its significant influence on their lives, be it saving them from the streets or providing an avenue to live out their commitment to multi-income, generational and multiracial living.

Affordable housing has a long and bleak history. In her book which ignited a new generation of urban reformers, Jane Jacobs lamented that low-income housing projects had "become worse centers of delinquency,

vandalism and general social hopelessness than the slums they were supposed to replace."5 Low-income housing projects have been infamous for
cutting people off from their communities, limiting access to safe, green
space, increasing crime or fear of crime and being downright aesthetically depressing. Folsom/Dore is a beacon of hope amidst such history. It
resists the pitfalls of previous homeless housing, and instead provides an
antidote to the idea that exciting designs, aesthetically interesting spaces
and green buildings are reserved for the rich. The closed-in, darkened
spaces that characterize much affordable housing are challenged here
where each resident has immediate access to the outside via yards or balconies, where windows and skylights stream sunlight into hip interior
spaces designed to be livable as well as green. Some of these elements featured in this resident's description of his apartment at Folsom/Dore

> Right, they all have balconies. The top floors, I
> think, are the best, because like I said we have sky-
> lights. We have balconies. I have the loft. Um, my
> roommate has, you know you walk in — you walk
> right into the kitchen and straight ahead there is
> the balcony, but there is also like the living room
> area. And then to the right is my roommate's room.
> Now, the only bad part about this is you have to be
> close. There are only half walls and there are no
> doors. I mean there is a door to the bathroom, but
> there is no like doors, you know the loft is a half
> wall, and even his room is a half wall, but he has
> built this sliding door that gives him privacy. It's a
> nice place.

When describing the apartments, Nina said

> You don't feel closed in. There isn't much of a dif-
> ference between being in the building and being out
> in the world. When you leave to take a walk down
> to the coffee shop the only difference is solitude.

One couple, two gay men, former lovers and now best friends who have been together for eleven years, still feel the pressure of rental cost, but find Folsom/Dore a very desirable place to live. They told us, "we set up the loft as a second bedroom; it feels so modern and spacious, we don't feel like we're making do in a one-bedroom. We're proud of our home." Brian, whom we spoke to at length went on

> We needed a place right away. The rent is high for affordable housing. And that is an issue every month to get: my work is sporadic due to my health, and my roommate is on SSI. We pay $1250 a month. We live on the fourth floor, which is the best apartment I feel. You know, we have the skylights, we have the loft, and he gets some help with Catholic Charities, a few hundred dollars a month, which we split.

The idea of a home and private space was not immediately understood or expected by many of the residents. Describing her moving day to Folsom/Dore one woman explained, "She gave me a key and all and then I said, 'let me in' and she said, 'Let yourself in, it's your apartment. You have the key.' I felt so good unlocking that door! It's mine. I live here."

While the apartments are built with the same emphasis on style and comfort as any other (non-affordable) housing project would be, the exterior spaces and communal areas also counter the assumptions and standards of the kinds of low-income housing projects soundly critiqued by Jane Jacobs and others. The architects designed an entry garden and stairwells as green open spaces to provide "a transitional decompression space between the homes and the hard urban environment outside." The main staircase is completely open and on every floor there is a breezeway, so there is always an outside element. Daniel Simons, the architect, described the importance of creating shades of public to private spaces to allow for neighbor interaction. "Intermediate spaces between public and private are important to foster feelings of comfort," he stated; at Folsom/Dore "we created shades from public to private and a full range in between."

Fig 5.6: *Playground at Folsom/Dore Apartments.*

A shared green space can be found in the building's inner courtyard. It hosts a playground and sitting area, and attention is given to the landscaping. Inside, communal spaces offer opportunities to socialize, meet with a case manager, utilize resident computers, pick up a car-share, access provisions offered by the local food bank or reserve space to hold a private event. One resident describes using the communal spaces to access computers

I was starting to use the computers. They had a bunch of computers in here ... I am not really computer

> savvy, so things happen when I touch the computer.
> So, I go to the library. But I thought it was so great
> to have the computers down here.

With access to shared facilities, Folsom/Dore not only enhances sustainability through sharing resources, it also realizes its goal of supporting and empowering residents to live independently. Building and maintaining community ties are often perceived as a luxury, and for many residents of Folsom/Dore, community has been formed in the street through drug use, violence, self-protection and sex work. Folsom/Dore is committed to changing these norms for its residents.

Overcoming the risks of violence, access to drugs and other safety concerns are constant issues for Folsom/Dore and its residents. While excited to be living at Folsom/Dore, one market-rate couple we spoke with discussed concern about living in an apartment building with formerly homeless residents (often with co-diagnoses): "I don't like to come home alone at night, but so far nothing has happened." They acknowledged that if you want to live in the heart of the city and benefit from the diversity, vibrancy and resources available, you have to find a way to balance safety with lifestyle.

While the reality of high crime in its surrounding neighborhood and residents' desires for safety necessitate bars and secure entrances, these things are done with a style that manages to avoid being foreboding and unwelcoming.[6] The building has stairwells with windows that were designed as public (i.e., open for use) for the residents, but the peripheral stairwells are alarmed, and residents are asked to use elevators and the central stairwell. This is a point of contention but also one that is an attempt to address security issues. One resident described his view of the need for security

> Well, I feel that although I have never been home-
> less, I believe there are people in the building that
> have gone from the streets to an apartment here.
> Um, I think the police are around here a lot; I think
> there are activities going on around here that

shouldn't be, but I think that you get that, well probably anywhere live ... They have security, which is good, very good. To have somebody down at the desk so people can't get into the building that don't belong here.

Lessons Learned from Folsom/Dore

Folsom/Dore represents the promise of addressing social needs with innovative architectural and engineering design. Residents at Folsom/Dore need housing, and many are committed to the social experiment of mixed-income supportive housing. Folsom/Dore can teach us how to address social needs without compromising individual human dignity or the significance that social connection and community can play in people's lives. Folsom/Dore is an example of a successful affordable housing building serving not only low-income, but formerly homeless and market-rate tenants. While examples of this have become more abundant, in 2001 the developers of Folsom/Dore faced numerous obstacles as few thought such a multi-purpose project could be done. They proved it could.

Folsom/Dore is also an example for how *sustainable community* needn't refer only to those that live in a particular place. Nina Berkson, Kevin Edelbrock and other staff members are not residents but have been a part of the Folsom/Dore community since its opening and have shown the residents a commitment not only to the conceptual ideas of social justice, but the concrete devotion to helping people to live lives with dignity, care from others and integration and interaction with neighbors and a neighborhood. Now that years have passed since the ribbon was cut by Mayor Newson at Folsom/Dore, some of the residents and support staff are looking forward to building an even greater sense of community involvement, planning events to build a community bound by this architectural structure. As Nina explained

> We've been having a lot of discussion recently around getting to a place where residents are ready to represent themselves. We've talked about putting

together art shows and other events that might
involve the neighborhood and outside community
and support the residents in their growth and
progress.

And in envisioning this community, the support staff and services
workers are part of that vision. When we spoke to Vernon, he described
mostly talking to the maintenance man and night manager: these were
the people who made his day. They were as important to Vernon as someone else's neighbors might be to them.

At this urban development, community expands to include the
Folsom/Dore staff, the social services workers and organizations that support the people who live there. We think this is a key point — because
it is not always enough to just assume that neighborly caregiving and
community support will emerge organically. Sometimes it does (as we
saw vividly at the cohousing communities we visited), but it would be a
mistake to depend on such spontaneous care to meet the needs of vulnerable populations. In planning Folsom/Dore, the developers integrated
caregiving into their plans by bringing in support services.

Finally, we think an important lesson at Folsom/Dore is the way in
which green features are seamlessly built into the building. As we have
discussed, many of the residents we spoke to do not even realize they live
in a green building. For us, the fact that people don't move there in order
to live green doesn't take away from the power or importance of sustainability. In fact, Folsom/Dore provides a window into a future where all
buildings are designed green, and sustainable living is merely a taken-for-
granted part of everyday life. Indeed, most of us don't spend very much
time thinking about where our energy comes from or what's off-gassing
from our carpets or furniture or what kind of toxic dust the skeleton of
our house is generating. The fact that these kinds of questions may not
be occurring to all of the residents at Folsom/Dore speaks to how seamless green design can be. For these residents, environmental sustainability
has been almost invisibly integrated into everyday life.

Part 3

Personal Choice —
Living Green as Individuals

A Love Affair — the Cazadero Nature and Art Conservancy

Here, we tell the story of Margaret Fabrizio and the nature and art conservancy which she has created amidst meadows and madrone trees in Northern California. This story is unique both for its focus on one individual's relationship to her land as well as for the contours of that relationship. While Margaret treads lightly on the land, she does so as an artist not an environmentalist. Not that these two things are separate. Indeed, as we talked to Margaret and visited her land, it is clear how closely intertwined they are. At Margaret's land we saw living green emerging out of an intimate love between an artist and a landscape. Hers is a practice that views landscape, not as something out there and separate from us, but as something inextricably linked to us.

In 1986 upon returning from a trip abroad, Margaret Fabrizio went to visit fellow travelers and a property they recommended. So began the story of the Cazadero Nature and Art Conservancy. Margaret refers to this site as *The Land*; and although she also thinks of it as the Cazadero Nature and Art Conservancy, as she tells us, Cazadero is the shaded, foggy and usually wet town below. The Land, in contrast, is a multi-terrained landscape that serves as her playground for whimsy and appreciation. The Land includes a large, open, sun-drenched meadow overlooking the valley, hillsides and various forested areas sloping downward and encircling the property.

Fig. 6.1: *Stelae in Front of Forest.*

The Land was purchased as an off-the-grid 40-acre parcel. It had not been lived upon by humans since Pomo people inhabited the area centuries ago. While miles from anything, The Land is officially located in the town of Cazadero, on the Sonoma Coast in the Russian River area of Northern California. The area is often described as a magical place of redwoods, rain and fog. There is little to do — no hotels, few stores, no downtown — just redwood forests, creeks and the Russian River. Upon her arrival, Margaret fell in love with this solitude and beauty as well as the opportunity it provided. It is a love affair she still nurtures over 20 years later.

Margaret Fabrizio

Fiercely independent and driven by artistic expression, Margaret has been well-known throughout her life as a pianist, harpsichordist, teacher, quilter

Fig. 6.2: *Margaret and Art Installation.*

and painter. She is now in her late seventies and divides her time each year between her home in San Francisco, The Land and trips to India.

Margaret began studying piano just before her third birthday. As a young adult she became a well-known harpsichordist playing concerts across America and Europe with musicians as diverse as the San Francisco Symphony and the Grateful Dead. She was on the faculty at Stanford University for 25 years. Throughout this career, she was active in multi-media: she performed in multi-image projections/harpsichord performances across Europe. Her compositions for solo harpsichord known as "Holograms" have been performed in America and abroad. In her home town of San Francisco, she has performed or exhibited her work at the city's most notable venues including the Museum of Modern Art, the Opera House, the de Young Museum, the Palace of Fine Arts and the Legion of Honor.

After 1980 Margaret became more active as a visual artist. Many of her collage works are in private collections; her Portrait Masks have been exhibited as far away as Edinburgh, Scotland and her travel books have been the focus of a special exhibit at the San Francisco History of The Book. Margaret studied quilt making with Grace Earl, Professor of Design at the Art Institute of Chicago, and Margaret's prize-winning quilts were exhibited at New Pieces Gallery in Berkeley where she also played a fortepiano concert.[1] Today, she continues an active artistic agenda producing works in these and other visual art media.

Traveling to The Land

On our first trip to The Land we were certain we were lost. Our city car barely made it up the steep, rocky and quite narrow road leading to the peak of the mountain. The winding road had been dotted with a few homes below, but for a long stretch no markers or houses appeared. When the road led to a small clearing and then narrowed even further up the mountain side, we thought we must have passed the house. Not allowing ourselves to second guess Margaret's directions, we continued up a dirt road for what felt like miles. At the top, another open site emerged marked with a small metal fence standing by a pull-out. We parked our car next to an old red pickup truck and walked across a clearing toward the woods. We noticed a few people up a hill but they didn't look toward us and we recognized no one, so we continued following what we believed to be a path. Soon, we came upon a small structure; not more than ten feet by five feet. It had a sturdy glass door, and when we peered inside we saw built-in storage, a bed and signs of recent activity. After a few moments as we headed away from the structure we heard footsteps behind us and there was Margaret walking away from us up a path toward the group we had originally dismissed as unrelated. We turned and followed. "Is this it?" we asked each other, "Are we here?"

For the past 25 years, The Land as a built environment has gradually developed. But this is not a project measurable by any of the green building rating systems available. There is no house on The Land. Instead, Margaret has created an environment organically over the years through a process of interaction and experimentation with landscape. First came an oversized four-poster bed constructed from discarded electric poles. The bed sits at the pinnacle of the meadow and overlooks the valley. When she sleeps there, Margaret drapes the bed with netting to protect her from mosquitoes. Over the years she has created, by hand, walking trails through the forested areas. She cleared sites to construct a wilderness stage, and she cuts the meadow grass yearly by hand.

Margaret Fabrizio

Fig. 6.3: *Margaret in Front of Glas Haus.*

When Margaret began living with The Land in 1986, she was drawn to the hillside, meadow views and vegetation — mostly ferns, rocks, madrone trees and some large oaks. When we first started talking with Margaret for this book, she described her relationship with The Land

> When I first started coming up here it was like a love affair. When I would get to the bottom of the road and start driving up my heart would start beating faster and I was going to meet my lover, you know, it felt just like that ... Like any love affair it changes with time, and pretty soon I had to get farther up that mountain before I would get that rush.

In 1986 The Land had no water. "It still has no water," she told us when we talked. We didn't have a chance to ask why before she explained, "I could put energy into developing those things. But for some reason or other, I have never been able to equate those kinds of activities with my love for The Land. I am deeply in love with it. It is just a treasure." There is electricity, something that took many years to arrange. The day the electricity was connected, Margaret had a celebration party with invited guests. Twenty years later at an anniversary celebration for The Land, a friend recounted the electricity party Margaret hosted. "I remember Margaret carrying a blender across the meadow to the houselette. She made margaritas in celebration." Although she comes with friends, mostly Margaret comes to Cazadero with her love for The Land and the artistic expressions it inspires.

Art and The Land: Collaborating with Nature

Visiting The Land, we were immediately drawn in by its beauty and openness. It is easy to see how an artist might view it as a natural canvas. As the seasons change, wind and rain transform the landscape. Margaret watches and then participates in the movements of the seasons, times of day and occasional human interactions.

Similar to environmentalists, Margaret wants to tread lightly. She brings only the materials she can carry or wheel from her car and leaves with her trash. She leaves as little a footprint as possible. More significantly, we think, she is an engaged witness in the way time and space flow through this landscape. She listens to The Land, its cycles, its heartbeat: at times she is drawn to respond and interact with it and at other times it demands that she do so. As a result of both natural occurrences and Margaret's vision, The Land has changed as works of art have been installed, as the wind or rain have taken them away and as the weather or disease transformed the natural habitat.

Margaret is highly driven. She has spent her life planning and achieving the goals she set for her art, career and travel. The Land, however, provides a very different space for her. As she describes it, she doesn't work at The Land; she plays there, watching and waiting for inspiration to come from her love and its love for her. "It's whimsy ... it's play ... it's not permanent. It was never about having any thing permanent," she explained. "It is a playground." She added, "I would just move all those rocks and after a few weeks or years" she continued, her voice raising to a high pitch, "Oh no, I think I'll put them into towers instead of walls. Since I never used cement I can move them over here. I can do these fun things. It never felt like work ..." In these descriptions, there is very little distinction between art and land.

We do not imply that Margaret views The Land as a mere tool for her creations. Indeed, it is very much the opposite. Margaret describes her relationship with The Land as one of reciprocity and collaboration. In Margaret's descriptions, The Land is animated with its own will.

> I might be away for a few months, and it is like when you left your pet cat and you come home and it won't even look at you [she turns dismissively]. So I felt The Land suddenly withdrew from me. And then I realized it was a reciprocating relationship: .... It wasn't just me loving The Land. The Land loved me.

Such interaction is another way of living in stewardship and respect for a natural environment. Margaret understood that she had to cultivate this relationship. Landscape is not something you sit passively with nor is it something you conquer and change, but something with which to interact in a non-harmful manner. And, because of this deep connection, the inevitable loss and regeneration of the natural world features in Margaret's art. For example, one of her installations explores the loss of a grove of madrones to sudden oak illness.

> The most major thing that has happened is that all the madrone trees have died. And they were real presence there. That's been a growth experience for me. It's just like the world. Trees die. It just happens. Trees fall down. There are always trees falling down. The first ten to twelve years I was here every fallen tree was a personal insult. If you are there long enough you realize Trees Fall Down. But the suddenness and completeness of these madrones going has really devastated the area ... So I made these PVC pipe cylinder things that I sank in the ground that would be steady. Then I could carry those big pieces of trees and stand them up. I did that in the meadow. So you got what were very large branches on huge trees which now they look like trees themselves cause they are standing up in cylinders. But I am kind of phasing that out; I think it served its purpose. It was kind of like a memorial to those trees.

Most of her installations, however, are not guided by intent. They are usually spontaneous expressions guided by an impulse that arrives as she watches, listens and thinks about the contours of the landscape. One story she shared with us was her *cleanup* of a fallen tree. When one tree fell it damaged the trunk of another, creating a dramatic sculptural effect that Margaret was driven to disentangle and investigate. She pulled and moved branches, rocks, twigs and large debris until the standing trunk came into clear view. Many of us might see this as work, but for Margaret it was a process of creation.

In a more sustained installation titled *Guardian Grove*, Margaret affixed paintings to several trees that constituted a grove. The grove itself provided the inspiration for the protection offered by the guardians she installed on some of the trees. A watchful eye — a blue, Turkish glass ball — hung from one tree to watch over the land. The guardians themselves, large-scale painted totemic figures inspired by the color palette of the grove as well as the scale and shape of each tree, embraced the landscape providing an ephemeral feel and another protective layer. In shadow and light, the guardians protect and watch over the land and its inhabitants.

Art installations are not always formal, however. The smaller acts of moving a stone, assembling debris or piling rocks are examples of the constant activities of engagement Margaret might do on any given day. She often brings materials given by friends or brought from her city home — a sculpture, a large swath of fabric or a found object — and places these within the landscape in a way that creates a shift in how she sees, experiences and makes sense of The Land.

Fig. 6.5: *Guardian Grove Installation.*

Adding Small Structures

While The Land, for Margaret, provides a canvas for art, shelter was another matter. "No matter what happens, seeing it {The Land} as material for art is much more interesting to me than building a house" she exclaimed. It is the love affair that directed her desire to live as lightly on The Land as possible. "That is why I didn't want to put a house on it. It seems so arrogant. Here is this precious spot on the planet, and I want to go put a house on it? For one thing, I didn't want to look at it … If you put one stick up it changes everything."

While there are several built structures at The Land — a stucco yurt, a gazebo, a houselette and her latest Clef House (used as a piano room and kitchenette) — housing is decidedly not what makes this landscape home for Margaret Fabrizio. During one of our conversations Margaret told us that living on The Land never

Margaret Fabrizio

Margaret Fabrizio

Fig. 6.6: *Yurt in Forest.*

felt like work. But when she continued this thought she said, "except when I tried to do construction. That was always work. There was always anxiety ... you wanted them to not leak, and there were always problems." She continued to describe her main house, the houselette

> You know, I have that tiny little house [8 x 12 feet].
> You don't have to walk in a house. If you have everything you need you can stand in one position. There are a stove top and microwave and bed and storage ... If I want to walk I can go outside. I am very happy with that.

Being inside is not what drew Margaret to The Land, yet as she ages she is finding herself spending increased time inside the houselette and other structures. Although this is less desirable, she is living with The Land in a new way, observing the areas closer to shelter in a more sustained manner. And as she told us, sometimes she too is observed by the wildlife that inhabit the land full-time.

The Side Effect of Social Connection

Our first visit to The Land was to attend the annual poetry festival, and knowing Margaret as we did, such an invitation was not something to pass up. Once we realized we were in the right place on this first visit, Margaret emerged from behind a small structure wearing an Indian sari and head wrap. She didn't say much nor did she introduce us to the other people quietly surrounding her. We had brought potato salad to share with the group, but when we did not see any kitchen or running water we knew this would not be an ordinary gathering. Margaret began to lead us across the meadow and down a stone path to what was recognizable as an amphitheater. It was apparent that she had created this space using natural elements of rock and stone, placing them along an upward-sloping hill. For the next hour or two each of her guests stood and read from either their books of published poetry or something written for the occasion. Margaret played music on a harmonium she had brought back from a recent trip to India.

Fig. 6.7: *Margaret in Front of Houselette.*

When we talked with Margaret about gathering people in this remote place, she said, "Connecting with people is a side effect. I just do my art. It is the art that I am interested in." Community is not something Margaret strives toward or believes in. It is not a word she would choose to use. However, she told us that she created the Cazadero Nature and Art Conservancy as a place to share with others who valued art, nature and The Land. It is the commitment to art that inspires her to invite others to share and gather. Over the 20 or more years she has been coming to this place, Margaret has held Easter gatherings, hosted the poetry festival, brought guests for weekend stays and recently held a 20-year anniversary party for The Land. But these gatherings, she reminded us frequently, are not her purpose.

Human-Environment Connection

As sociologists, we have been trained to look for a theory that explains human actions even if these actions are complicated and messy. It is not surprising that the story of Margaret Fabrizio and the Cazadero Nature and Art Conservancy elides easy explanation. We could have concluded that Margaret's vision developed out of radical youth responses to the conservative 1950s and 1960s. In fact, Margaret had flirted with the countercultural movements that existed in the late 1950s through the 1970s in North America. She knew many beatniks, feminists, draft dodgers, artists and others who chose to drop out of mainstream culture and live according to their own ideals. But theirs were not the guiding principles Margaret lived by. She was building a reputation as a world-class musician; countercultural activities were experiences she fit in en route to and from her concerts.

It is individualism made anew through personal self-expression central to many of these counter cultural practices that resonate in Margaret's relationship with The Land. In fact, she tells a great story about her trip in the very early 1970s to Ken Kesey's farm in Oregon. She was touring as a harpsichordist and, she told us, she "thought she would stop by and see what would happen." This approach is not unusual for Margaret. Being a part of any movement is not what Margaret is about. As much as we wanted to position her within a social movement, doing so would not clarify Margaret and her relationship with The Land even though, in some ways, her time on The Land exists in symbiosis with those who dropped out of mainstream culture along the Northern coast of California and Oregon.

It was also in the late1960s and early 1970s that a land art movement formed in the United States in which landscape and art were viewed as linked.[2] For these artists, sculptures and other art forms are not placed on or in the landscape; rather the landscape was the raw material and means

Margaret Fabrizio

of the art form. Once produced, the work of art was understood to be temporal, open to change and erosion from natural conditions of the weather and cycle of the day (e.g., ice melting in afternoon sun, a sculpture eroding at high tide). Similar to youth countercultural practices, land artists were also reacting against commercialism and conservative tenets of the historical time in general and the art world more specifically. Refusing the museum as an institution and art as a commodity and permanent form, many artists developed projects beyond the reach of these established cultural worlds.

Yet the land art movement, like counterculturalism, does not explain Margaret's relationship with The Land. Both provide a backdrop of the Northern California political, art, and social climate within which Margaret's love affair unfolded but they were not inspirations for what Margaret was doing. When she heard about the British landscape artist Andy Goldsworthy,

Fig. 6.8: *Wood Wall Art Installation.*

Margaret Fabrizio

Fig. 6.9: *Clef House in Meadow.*

for example, it was in the 1990s.[3] "It was validating" she told us. "When I finally saw Goldsworthy it was like a validation of the considerable *meaning* of what I was doing up there, just playing ….. Suddenly I felt it deserved some respect … it gave it a validation. It wasn't just me." Her art is also site specific and utilizes materials from the environment in a way that brings out the changing character of the place. The materials are most often natural and found objects (i.e., rocks from the old logging road or branches cut down from dead trees) that she arranges into temporary sculptures, at times adding objects and art from the cultural world as well.

Margaret's actions embrace a deep respect and admiration for other living things. She lives in a way that understands that she is part of nature. Her relationship with the natural world tells her — and all of us — who we are and where we belong. Her memorial to the fallen trees began with the assertion that "we all die;" over time she came to understand these deaths as part of a larger cycle and truth.

Margaret continues to live in unison with The Land, understanding that nothing exists in isolation from or disconnected from any other thing. The spiritual connection she feels with The Land, for us, is itself a lesson that there are many ways to express green awareness and be environmentally sensitive. Margaret did not tell us that for her humans emerged from, are embedded in and are dependent upon nature and other forms of life for our well-being and survival. This is not an idea that drives her action. Yet, it appears to be a taken-for-granted truth that shapes her love affair with The Land. She exists in connection, not taking but engaging in a balanced and reciprocal relationship with The Land. While community is not a word Margaret uses to describe the social world, it does seem that she sees herself in a community of living things.

During one of our conversations Margaret expressed her dream that The Land continue as a nature and art conservancy. She has not had the energy to develop this into its full potential, but she envisions a place where artists and people who appreciate art can come and do their art. She envisions Cazadero as a shared space in the future. The poetry festival, art installations and group gatherings have each and all been part of building the conservancy into an outdoor gallery. "It's all about sharing. That's the main thing. I don't feel that this place is mine. I don't feel I have any right to hog it all, and I feel I want people to have a chance." She completed our interview by saying in her visionary and generous way, "This is what this could be."

Mainstream Green

MOST NORTH AMERICANS RECOGNIZE THE NEED TO LIVE in more environmentally and socially sustainable ways. People everywhere are doing their part to reduce energy consumption, to recycle plastics and paper, to use fewer chemicals and to generally live their lives in more Earth-friendly ways. Many of the practices emphasized in the communities showcased thus far are indeed shared by a growing majority of the North American public: a yearning for and use of green spaces, an urban interest in car-sharing, a reduction of personal energy consumption and an overall concern for the future of our planet.

Alongside this growing interest, a vibrant green building movement has emerged to offer sustainable building and renovation options to meet this growing demand for more sustainable living options for the mainstream. Most North Americans don't live in ecovillages or communes, but rather in single family homes and multi-family apartments or condominiums. So, what does it take to emphasize environmental and social sustainability in mainstream residential living practices? What are the alternatives for single-family and multi-unit dwellings for the majority of North Americans? We turn to two innovative North American examples for living green: architect Michelle Kaufman's prefabricated green single-family homes and the Dockside Green development in British Columbia.

Greening the Nuclear Family Home

In 2006 the National Building Museum in Washington DC had a special exhibit called "The Green House: New Directions in Sustainable Architecture and Design." With other visitors, we entered the exhibit directly onto the deck stairs of a prefabricated house featuring dual-paned, energy efficient sliding glass doors and windows, exterior warm wood shutters (sunshades) in straight, clean lines, clerestory windows allowing cross ventilation, bamboo floors, a kitchen designed for modern living with open counter and high quality, energy efficient appliances. Signs were placed throughout the house pointing to the energy efficient materials, water-saving plumbing fixtures, healthy finishes (such as non-toxic paints and formaldehyde-free cabinets) and myriad other elements of green design incorporated into this dwelling. This house was called the Glidehouse, and it is one of several prefabricated green homes designed by Michelle Kaufmann.

In many ways entering the house, erected inside the Building Museum, felt similar to going to an open house — an activity that became

Fig. 7.1: *Interior of Glidehouse*tm *by Michelle Kaufmann Designs.*

John Swain

a recreational pastime during the housing bubble of the early 21st century. This open house, however, seemed different. People were inquiring about the materials used in the building's design, the size of the truck needed to transport it and the ways one might site the home to take advantage of morning sun. The onlookers' curiosity about issues rarely brought forward in the buying and selling of mainstream real estate stood out.

After exiting the house, a large flat-screen video monitor continuously played an image of a young architect walking slowly and seamlessly from the interior to the exterior of this same house. As she crossed the sliding doors onto the sustainable decking, she leaned over a railing and glanced at a Northern California sunset. We were transported from a museum exhibit below sea level in Washington, DC to the personal residence of Michelle Kaufman in the Bay Area of California. It was quite a ride — you could smell the breeze.

Michelle Kaufmann has emerged as a strong advocate for bringing eco-friendly living to greater numbers of people by using pre-packaged

Fig. 7.2: Glidehousetm by Michelle Kaufmann Designs.

John Swain

green solutions in building designs. Previously an associate for architect Frank Gehry in Los Angeles, Kaufmann moved to the San Francisco Bay area with her husband and found herself unable to find a home that she both liked and could afford. Dissatisfied with a lack of sustainability offered by either suburban developments or the quality of housing found in urban fixer-uppers, she and her husband decided to buy some land and build their own house — a quintessentially American ideal. Yet, innovation was central. In her building, she brought to life her concept of sustainability: modular building utilizing smart technology and eco-friendly design principles.

The first modular house was designed for her and her husband and sited on a Northern California hillside outside of San Francisco. When we asked her how she liked it, Michelle replied

> I love my home. I love that it's relatively small but feels so spacious thanks to its connection to the beautiful California countryside. I love the light. I also love that we are drastically reducing our consumption of natural resources. Our energy bills are $0, and according to our latest water bill, we use 70% less water than our neighbors.

In 2002, she founded her own firm in Oakland California — Michelle Kaufmann Designs (mkDesigns) — and took her plans into factory production. Her first project was to build her home on site and then compare the time and material waste it took to do so with that of building the very same home in a factory. The factory won. Today, mkDesigns offers several models of homes which are built in factories, transported and buttoned-up almost anywhere. These are prefabricated, but can be personalized to fit the living needs of buyers.

Prefabricated homes have always offered potential for low-cost, efficiency and predictability in building designs. The eminent architect and affordable housing guru, Avi Friedman, described some of the advantages of prefabrication in his book *Room for Thought*. According to Friedman, prefabrication holds the potential for high quality homes that can be flexibly catered to the needs of the people for whom they're designed. Prefabrication is efficient and enables building in diverse climates, under varying conditions and at less cost. It also substantially reduces waste produced at the work site.

Yet, as Friedman described, despite attempts by companies such as Sears and Roebuck throughout the 19th century to offer mail-order homes, only 10% of all North American homes are currently built in a factory. This is in sharp contrast to other countries. At the opposite extreme, in Sweden 90% of all homes are prefabricated. It seems that in North America prefab is still associated with cheap and aesthetically displeasing architecture. But with modular preconfigured design that association is changing.

The change in attitude to prefab seems to be driven by two forces: an appreciation of design and the need to find positive solutions to increasing environmental and climate crises. These are joined with an increasing consumer demand to live more eco-friendly lives. Michelle Kaufmann and her associates stand out for their unique approach to melding prefabricated modular homes with a goal of living green — and doing it all with a high regard for style. Far from the trailer park image of prefab, Kaufmann's homes are high design, modern residences with wide appeal. As described on the mkDesigns website, her prefrabricated homes follow five "principles of eco-friendliness and cost effectiveness, without sacrificing beauty."

Like other green designs, the dwellings offered by mkDesigns adhere to the LEED rating system, and each structure achieves either a platinum or gold rating depending on the personal choices made by the residents concerning size, finishes and site. There are currently six designs to choose from. Each is preconfigured in factory-built modules and is built as a single family dwelling designed for various environments from city to rural and with different site and size needs in mind. The firm also offers custom projects. As of summer 2008, mkDesigns had completed 28 dwellings with over 300 more in the pipeline. One of these is a 2 bedroom, 2 bathroom Glidehouse built in the mountains of Ukiah, California for Kim and Conie. Kim told us, "This home provides us nothing more than what is needed. It's smaller, more self-sufficient. The green building

JB Spector

Fig. 7.3: *Placing the mkSolaire*ᵗᵐ *smart home on site.*

technologies just blew us away." Even when space is abundant, many homeowners like Kim and Conie are finding that a small footprint makes sense. The seamlessness of interior to exterior maximizes living space and proximity to the outdoors.

In addition to the single family market, mkDesigns has recently expanded into multi-unit modular green housing developments and has two new projects underway: a townhouse development in Northern California and a community design project in Denver, Colorado. Kaufmann said

> We believe that with the right thinking and imple-
> mentation, green housing can be for the masses, and
> it should be! That is what drives all of our work
> every day. It is also a big reason why we are working
> with developers on communities of both single fam-
> ily and multi-family projects.

Bringing mkDesigns designs to the masses will address not only environmental and design needs, but will also lower the cost of building these modular homes. While a single family dwelling can cost $250 per square foot to build (excluding the land), it is estimated that a multi-family dwelling project will cost $150-160 dollars per square foot. This will increase affordability. In addition, the move into community development is a recognition of the increasing sustainability that density and proximity can offer residents.

While Michelle Kaufmann is working to bring a new era to prefabricated homes, the legacy of prefabrication and single-family housing continues to be felt in the ongoing North American problems with suburban sprawl — lack of public transportation and over reliance on cars, living in racially segregated towns and communities, living with increased environmental pollution and decreased tolerance for non-traditional expression.

Green Housing for the Masses:
Rethinking Little Boxes on a Hillside

At the same time as B.F. Skinner was dreaming his utopia in *Walden Two* and inspiring a generation of back-to-the-landers, William Levitt was inspiring a revolution in the opposite direction. A confluence of factors in the post-war period of the United States caused demand for housing to swell to previously unknown proportions, and a housing shortage was the result. One factor was financing: the US government, in the wake of the great depression, created the Federal Housing Administration to help people finance home ownership. This opened up the possibility, the very idea, of home ownership to groups of people who previously wouldn't have been considered candidates. Further, the GI bill concretized the notion that all returning soldiers should have access to home ownership. These governmental interventions, coupled with post-war prosperity and burgeoning population, led to high demand for houses. And the building industry was not keeping up.

In the 1940s, housebuilding was still dominated by small, locally owned firms, and construction was small-scale. Beginning in the 1950s, this changed dramatically. The housebuilding industry grew exponentially, and the rate of production followed suit. Large building companies began taking advantage of prefabrication, standardized dimensions and mass production.

At the forefront of these post WWII changes was the firm Levitt and Sons and their Levittown developments (the most prominent in Pennsylvania, New Jersey and Long Island). William Levitt began experimenting with prefabricated designs during the war in an effort to create low-cost housing; while not the first to do so, his firm was perhaps the most successful at the time. Applying the logic of assembly-line production to house-building, he rapidly increased the pace at which houses could be built, developing identical houses in uniform rows on increasingly larger swaths of land. Materials and supplies were pre-assembled whenever possible, packaged and brought to the location where builders assembled them. Levitt liked to call his company the "General Motors of the housing industry."[1] To keep down lumber costs, the Levitts bought their own forests and built a sawmill in Oregon. They purchased appliances directly from manufacturers, cutting out the distributor's markup. They even made their own nails.

When William Levitt completed the building of Levittown, Pennsylvania in 1958, it was the largest development ever built by a single builder and the first truly master-planned community: it included residential areas separated by playgrounds and parks, schools and roads. It also utilized cost-efficient, factory production in its bottom line. These mass-produced homes were built at a rate of roughly 40 per day and, doing this made homeownership affordable for middle- and working-class people.

While opening up home ownership for some, Levittown suburbs also helped perpetuate inequalities. Barring home ownership in Levittown for non-whites, the Levittown Racial Exclusion Clause stated: "The tenant agrees not to permit the premises to be used or occupied by any person other than members of the Caucasian race. But the employment and maintenance of other than Caucasian domestic servants shall be permitted." Levitt was not the only developer to enforce such a law. Most designed communities of the late 19th and early 20th centuries were created with the very same racist policies. While not all proponents supported racial covenants, most advocated economically exclusionary restrictions on property, such as minimum house sizes or costs, the exclusion of home businesses and mandatory architectural review.[2] Yet, a different picture of suburbia is evident today. Today, suburbia is home to more people than cities and rural areas put together. *Metroburbias*, sprawling city-towns, are occupied by new immigrants, increasing numbers of African-Americans, gays and the poor. Single people and the elderly outnumber married couples with children.[3] As Dolores Hayden documented in her book, *Building Suburbia*, the suburbs are as dynamic as cities: neither their social meaning nor their architectural form can be summed up by the white picket fence.

Master-planned communities like Levittowns were also major contributors to the environmental problems of suburban sprawl, quickly replicating throughout North America communities based on car ownership, individualized space and energy-intensive lifestyles. Suburbia and its sprawl into rural areas cannot be ignored by the green building movement. And, indeed, it isn't. Increasingly, the recognition has emerged that sustainable innovations in housing must include everything from the gated rural community and student housing options in a Kentucky university to the new urbanism of downtown Chicago and other cities as well as everything in between.

Newland Communities is one of the leading residential community developers in North America; it is also an innovator in sustainable building practices. Newland has recently implemented a project aimed at bringing sustainable principles to master-planned suburban communities. Newland's Healthy Living Systems strategy will deliver sustainable communities on a larger scale. This is achieved through careful siting, preservation of greenspace and green building practices for all homes constructed. Healthy Living Systems is a mixed-use plan which includes a village center and civic as well as commercial amenities.[4] In this way, Newland Communities is planning future projects that will provide an alternative to dominant practices. Newland is one of many mainstream developers using the LEED for Homes rating system.[5] Jerry Yudelson cites Shea Homes in San Diego, the tenth largest builder in the United States, as an example of where the mainstream house building market is heading. "Shea developed a package of energy conservation and solar technologies in 2001. Their new product line, the High Performance Home, meets the requirements of an Energy Star home, meaning it is designed to expend 15% less energy on heating, cooling and water heating than a similar home built to 2004 International Residential Code standards."[6]

Governments are taking bold steps as well. In July 2008 California's Building Standards Commission became the first jurisdiction in the US to require green building practices in all new construction, including single family homes, with its adoption of the California Green Building Standards Code. The code requires green building features for all new construction. It includes air quality, moisture control and resource conservation standards; the use of low- or no-volatile organic compound adhesives, paints and coatings; high-efficiency air conditioning filters and always-on exhaust fans to ensure better fresh air circulation in the home and new water-use standards that will require a 20% reduction in overall water use. The new standards take effect July 1, 2009, and will be phased in over the course of several years. The standards are predicted to make new homes in the state 50% more energy efficient than homes built to existing national energy standards.[7]

Thinking Beyond Single-Family Homes: Redesigning Neighborhoods

In general, North American building standards are fast moving toward higher density, mixed use, greater diversity in building materials and choices, increased environmental friendliness and other inherently green practices. Green buildings are springing up in downtown urban areas and suburban developments.

The natural devastation brought to New Orleans and other Gulf Regions as well as the town of Greensburg, Kansas have generated large-scale green building efforts. Greensburg, for example, the town completely destroyed by a tornado in May 2007, has been rebuilt as a model green community. All city buildings greater than 4,000 square feet are to be certified LEED Platinum, making this rural community the first city in the US to adopt LEED for an entire community. BNIM Architects of Kansas City, Missouri, worked with the city to draft the new building standards.[8]

At the residential level in New Orleans, Global Green USA responded to the aftermath of Hurricane Katrina by spearheading a series of green building projects with the first one targeting affordable housing reconstruction in the devastated ninth ward. The Holy Cross Project was launched with funding from the Home Depot Foundation. This was followed by a Green Schools Initiative, a policy agenda and a green building resource center. Actor Brad Pitt, in collaboration with Global Green USA and Habitat for Humanity, led an effort to build over 100 homes in New Orleans using green building guidelines.

New Urbanism has been an important force in building greener communities. New Urbanists Andres Duany and Elizabeth Plater-Zyberk began developing communities that were meant to model village life — they were mixed-use, near transportation and walkable and so countered the suburban trend of dependence on a car. The idea was being able to walk to things, to see your neighbors and to access resources.[9] As Jerry Yudelson has said, "a mixed-use revolution is underway."

Reflecting these trends, the Congress for New Urbanism, together with the USGBC and the Natural Resource Defense Fund, launched LEED for Neighborhood Development (LEED-ND). LEED-ND provides guidelines and standards for creating green communities, not just buildings. The LEED-ND rating system places value on green building practices coupled with principles of smart growth and new urbanism. The ideas mirror many already being incorporated into innovative master-planned communities: reducing urban sprawl, encouraging healthy living, protecting threatened species, increasing transportation choice and decreasing automobile dependence as well as high-performance green technologies and buildings.

The future of planned green communities may have already been realized at Dockside Green. Dockside Green is a 15-acre, master-planned harborfront community on a former brownfield site in Victoria, British Columbia. Dockside Green sprang out of a partnership between Vancity Credit Union — Canada's largest credit union, internationally well-known for innovative community programs — and Windmill West, a recognized North American leader in green building and community design. Busby, Perkins + Will were the architects for the project. When complete, Dockside Green will include three distinct neighborhoods, each a mixed-use array of residences, green spaces, offices, retail and commercial properties. Its stated vision reads like a textbook for social sustainability

> Dockside Green will be a socially vibrant, ecologically restorative, economically sound and just community. It will be a distinct collection of beautifully designed live, work, play and rest spaces designed to enhance the health and well-being of both people and ecosystems, both now and in the future.[10]

In late 2008, Phase I of Dockside was nearing completion, and the first residents had moved in. At first glance, Dockside is similar to other trendy downtown new developments cropping up in urban centers like

Fig. 7.4: *Joe Van Bellegham in Front of Dockside Green.*

Dockside Green

Vancouver, Seattle, Chicago or New York. Architects Busby, Perkins + Will created a sleek and appealing design, coupling density with ample greenspace and magnificent views.

What you might not guess just by looking is that Dockside is one of the greenest communities in North America. It was the first master-planned development to target LEED Platinum certification. In making such a commitment, the developer has agreed to face financial penalty if the project doesn't meet its goals. Fortunately, Dockside Green has: when it met that goal for its first phase in July 2008, it achieved the highest rating in the world at the Platinum level in the category of new construction. Out of a total 70 points possible — for things like water efficiency, sustainable site, energy and atmosphere, indoor air quality and innovation in design — Dockside Green achieved 63 points.

Sustainable Building Practices at Dockside Green

So, what makes Dockside so green? According to developer Joe Van Bellegham, one of the masterminds behind the community, it isn't that what they are doing at Dockside is so innovative in and of itself, but that they have taken the best innovations from all over the green building world and put them together in the same place for the first time.

One such innovation is a biomass plant. Currently in development, the renewable energy plant will use waste wood biomass to produce a clean gas for heating and hot water. This will make Dockside Green the first community-level development to be greenhouse gas positive from an energy perspective. Dockside Green utilizes a distributive system for all services: energy, water, waste, sewage are all dealt with on a community scale.

Another innovation is found in Dockside's approach to water conservation. Located on the city harborfront with spectacular views of one of the most beautiful waterways in North America, it is appropriate that Dockside emphasizes sustainable water in its design. From the start, the developers were committed to having on-site water treatment. Already committed to reducing water usage, having the on-site sewage plant created additional incentive to keeping water use down — the more water that's used, the more expensive it is to treat. To this end, all units include

Dockside Green

water-efficient fixtures such as dual flush toilets, 1.5 gpm showerheads, water efficient taps and high-efficiency dishwashers and washing machines. All the water that is used at Dockside will be treated on-site. The treated water will then be re-used on-site for things like flushing toilets, irrigation and for topping up ponds. In addition to water conservation, Dockside Green's approach to sewage will lower CO_2 emissions, as heat will be recovered from the sewage treatment process to heat buildings.

Green roofs and green wall features adorn the buildings at Dockside Green. The green roofs recycle water by directing overflow into rain cisterns on each resident's balcony, providing water for planters and houseplants. Water in excess of the cistern volume is directed to naturalized creeks and ponds that pepper the site. Instead of being directed there through pipes, however, it is carried via open channels. The purpose of this design is to enable residents, visitors and others to see the flow of water through the site — thus, it educates the public about how water is used and reused. Once water

Fig. 7.5: *Water at Dockside Green.*

arrives at the creeks and ponds, natural ecosystems clean and control it.

Energy efficient buildings are another way Dockside was developed to the LEED platinum standard. Their goal was to build 47% more efficiently than the Model National Energy Code specified, and they have thus far surpassed that goal. The builders understood how orientation impacts efficiency. Their passive design maximizes the power of the sun through strategic insulation, window panes, shades and building location. LED lighting, motion-sensor lighting in some areas and efficient appliances all are utilized to improve efficiency within units.

Photovoltaics, solar hot water products, native plants and trees, erosion and sedimentation control, shoreline rehabilitation, minimization of light pollution, environmentally-friendly products and building materials are all among the elements that make Dockside remarkably green. As impressive as these accomplishments are or are gearing up to be, what stood out about this community for us was the way it has integrated social sustainability into its design.

Living Dockside Green

From its outreach to the larger community, commitment to affordability, its walkability and human-scale design to its partnership with local First Nations, social concerns have been highlighted throughout the planning and execution of Dockside Green.

The design is oriented toward community-building. Principles of new urbanism maximize the potential for connectivity and neighborliness. The project is built to a human scale, it is close to downtown Victoria and consciously developed to get people walking, meeting each other and interacting. It is a mixed-use community — with retail, commercial, residential and recreational spaces co-mingling — in order to enhance vitality and to enable people to live a full life close to home.

Fig. 7.6: *Dockside Green Common Rooftop Garden.*

Melinda Jolley

One of the favorite gathering spots amongst the first wave of residents at Dockside is a community roof garden on one of the lower-rise buildings. There, residents have found an easy way to get to know each other while exchanging gardening tips and sharing the fruits of their labors. While the commercial units were not yet occupied when we spoke with residents, they were anticipating the imminent arrival of a fair-trade coffee shop and organic bakery. And, in the meantime, the harbor shuttle made runs to a local pub.

While Dockside includes high-end and market-rate properties, it also maintains a commitment to keep some of its units affordable in the long-term. Early on in its design, Dockside Green began integrating affordable housing into its overall vision. Currently, the design provides for 26 market-affordable units for ownership, targeting incomes between $30,000-$60,000. These will be sold with a strict covenant to ensure that they will continue to be sold below market rate in the future. The master plan for Dockside Green also includes 49 rental units, 70% of which will be two or three bedrooms in size.

In addition to maintaining affordable units, Dockside Green will provide free initial car share membership, a bicycle and a bus pass subsidy of $15/month for three years for up to 75 non-market and market affordable units. A number of market-affordable units will be made available to households making the jump into home ownership from subsidized rental housing, working with Vancity and its innovative green financing models.

Perhaps the most publicized aspect of Dockside's Green social ethic has been its First-Nations' job training program. In creating any sustainable community, the contours of the land — geography, ecology, culture and history— are all taken into account. Just as the average rainfall is something to be considered, so too are the cultural roots of any site.

Up until 1912, the Songhees and Esquimalt Nations lived sustainably on the land now home to Dockside Green. The development partners wanted to acknowledge and include this fact in their overall concept.

> [We] ... immediately sought to include these local Coast Salish nations in the planning for Dockside Green. With respect and honoring those that lived on the land before us, an awareness and educational process was initiated that resulted in numerous meetings, dialogue and ceremonies.[11]

A Memorandum of Understanding on Cooperation and Communication was signed by the developers and by the chiefs of the Songhees and Esquimalt Nations in October of 2006; this laid out some specific strategies

Dockside Green

Fig. 7.7: *Pole raising at Dockside Green.*

for connection. First, it was agreed that all parties would cooperate to develop Dockside Green "to ensure sustainable development in a manner respectful of the objectives and values of the Songhees Nation and Esquimalt Nation."[12]

More specifically, an agreement to promote understanding of First Nations' interests has led to participation in events, to a public art program where aboriginal art pieces are displayed at Dockside and to the integration of Songhees Nation and Esquimalt Nations' ceremonies in the key moments at Dockside Green. A job training and employment program was also implemented. The program includes First Nations job coaches who helped to train and integrate unemployed and underemployed First Nations people into trades and other jobs at Dockside Green. This program also supported skills acquisition to enhance future opportunities.

Another way that we see Dockside Green integrating the social side of sustainability into its design is in its emphasis on building for health. The recognition that built environments can play a critical role in the promotion of public health is evident at Dockside. This is true both in its location and in its buildings.

One of the strategies for health was to design each unit to receive 100% fresh air. This is a vast departure from mainstream practice. An air ventilation system pumps clean, fresh air into every dwelling and, as the air is exhausted, heat is recovered to pre-warm new incoming air. Additionally, to ensure indoor air quality, all the paints, sealants and adhesives are naturally sourced and eco-friendly with low- or no-VOC (volatile organic compounds) content. An independent test of indoor air quality is carried out before any tenants move into the building. Finally, each resident receives a six-month supply of green housekeeping supplies when they move to Dockside.

In addition to the focus on healthy buildings, Dockside Green encourages healthy lifestyles, maximizing local, health-enhancing features of the environment. The development is adjacent to a major bike trail network in Victoria and has seamlessly integrated itself into the existing framework while also making improvements. In order to encourage bike riding, bike lockers were built and a shower will be built so that people who work but don't live at Dockside will be able to bike to work.

Dockside resident Melinda Jolley described hopping on the Galloping Goose trail and riding to local farms to pick up something for dinner and then riding home to cook. It's hard to imagine a more splendid solution to public health problems resulting from bad diets and lack of exercise in North America.

People Make it Green

One of the things that Dockside Green has figured out is that you need people to make a green development work. You need commitment to change and to live differently. Dockside has done this in at least two ways. First, they have engaged the commitment from multiple constituencies throughout their development process. The project has exceeded expectations from both an ecological and an economic perspective, and the way people have rallied around the project has a good deal to do with that success. Second, Dockside Green has designed multiple mechanisms by which living green is made easier.

In describing what he was most proud of in the development of Dockside Green, Joe Van Bellegham said, "Unlocking the power of the triple bottom line." While Dockside is winning awards and breaking records for its green technologies, according to Joe, "You can't change the system unless you change people's minds." And, by truly integrating social along with ecological and economic concerns in every phase of the creation of Dockside, it seems minds have definitely been changed.

Joe went on to elaborate the power that he sees in the triple bottom line and why he is so proud of what they've accomplished at Dockside. It's remarkable that Dockside Green has managed to surpass expectations in terms of its environmental accomplishments, as well as do it affordably. According to Joe, they have managed to create such a watershed project at reasonable cost because a value shift has occurred. Programs like the First Nations job training and ambitious ecological targets have inspired people working on the project. Tradespeople, architects, engineers, developers, financers and community members — all of the various constituencies whose collaborative efforts are responsible for building a community — have developed a deep commitment to the project. Simultaneously, each person's commitment has helped them all become more deeply committed to sustainability. Joe said

> I have noticed that by truly being committed to sustainability and undertaking, for instance, the First Nations job training program, by getting our contractors to buy into a sustainable future we are engaging their hearts. We have the most amazing contractors and subtrades that are working with us to ensure we are successful. We are on budget and have had no problem getting labor. When I look at our own company, Dockside is outshining our other projects in large part because we are encouraging values in our consultants and contractors ... getting

them inspired about sustainability, having them
inspire us ... and the results are getting better.

Another way Dockside has recognized the power of people is by
designing a community that makes it easy and convenient to live more
lightly on the land. If, in the first instance, the achievement was to inspire
and motivate people to want to do it, here, the achievement has been to
make it so easy that people will do it.

Melinda Jolley was among the first wave of residents to move into
Dockside Green. In describing some of how it's different to live there,
Jolley remarked on various features that make it easier to live green.

> There's a carbon footprint monitor where you can
> see how much you are using by the day, week or
> month and can compare. Usually, it's kind of hard to
> see the difference it makes to turn off lights or to
> see the impact of having a bath versus a shower. It
> makes it easier to change your behavior with this
> information. I still love my baths, but I do take
> more showers now, knowing that they do use sub-
> stantially less water.

Melinda was referring to an individualized meter in every unit that
can tell you how much energy you personally are using. Her observations
have been backed up by research: studies indicate that people use substantially less energy and/or water when they are able to monitor their
own use and see the actual benefits of efforts to conserve.

To make things even easier, information on your personal meter can
be accessed over the Internet: you can compare your use with what you
used yesterday, last week or last year. You can also use the Internet to
remotely control heat, air conditioning and the exterior blinds in your
home. So, if you happen to be on vacation and can't remember if you
turned off the heat, you can check up on your energy consumption and
change settings inside your home from afar. Or, if a day turns unexpectedly sunny while you are at work, you can lift your blinds over the

Internet, thus using the solar energy to warm your home before you arrive.

Melinda has also found living car-free is possible because of having moved to Dockside Green. While she still owns her SUV, she decided to let her insurance lapse and to stop driving. Because of Dockside's central location and its car share program, Melinda felt it was easier to live car-free. While she moved from another central location, without the car share program that exists at Dockside not using her car just wasn't feasible before. Again, we see the meshing of values that green communities inspire: with the design features of a community (in this case, location and a car share program) enabling living in a greener way.

From an individual consumer looking for a home to a large-scale municipality passing a building ordinance, green building practices are fast becoming the norm. Dockside and other green building projects teach us that living green is going mainstream. And while it remains true that throughout North America individual home ownership has been emphasized as an essential indication of successful adulthood with high value placed on things like independence, private property, consumerism and nuclear family, these values are today joined with sustainability

Melinda Jolley

Fig. 7.8: *Melinda Jolley at Home at Dockside Green.*

demands. While cynics may believe that North Americans are too indi-
vidualistic to fully resonate with many of the green communities that we
have described here, people across the US and Canada are striving to live
more sustainable lives, and decades of a green building movement is today
poised to change our ways of living. Mainstream residential greening,
therefore, can and does offer solutions to the pressing environmental issues
of our time. As these examples demonstrate, the glass is half full: we need
to continue to seek ways that conserve energy and resources and live
lightly on the land and, when it becomes necessary to build and rebuild,
we need to turn to innovative sustainable design practices.

Lessons Learned:
The Ten Cs of Social Sustainability

IN A TIME OF INCREASING ENVIRONMENTAL BAD NEWS, it was heart-ening for us to witness the many ways people are working and living sustainably. As social science researchers, we set out to measure the best practices of sustainable residential design and to identify and understand the social mechanisms that most contribute to a sustainable community. We quickly realized, however, that we wanted to tell stories of the people and communities we visited. These places were full of promise and guidance for the future. They demonstrate that there is no single model for living green. It is a varied and widely divergent practice that can include innovative building designs or not building at all. Taken together, the sites presented here provide lessons for a more sustainable future. These places and the people who inhabit them challenge us to think differently about what constitutes community, healthy living and environmental sustainability.

The green building movement has incorporated the concept of the triple bottom line to assert that sustainable long-term progress in terms of environmental quality, economic development and social well-being needs to be balanced. One aspect cannot be emphasized over another. Yet the factors that best promote social well-being are the least understood. We return in this final chapter to our original goals as researchers: to identify and describe the mechanisms built into communities that most enhance social along with economic and environmental concerns. The examples showcased in this book collectively provide best practices: ten Cs of social sustainability. These practices emerged from the ground up through our talks with various members of communities, our interviews with planners, builders and architects and our study of community materials and social science literatures. The unique and groundbreaking projects can give us insight that can apply to any development The Ten Cs are

- Culture
- Context
- Citizenship
- Commitment
- Collaboration
- Connectedness
- Care
- Contact
- Commons
- Continuity

These findings are a first step in drafting more comprehensive guidelines for social sustainability. We offer these to developers of the projects of the future. They can be used in their meetings and charrettes, by community organizers during action initiatives and policy statements, by evaluators and process outcome researchers and by all those engaged in this "greatest movement no one ever saw coming" to again quote Paul Hawken.

1 – Culture

The first lesson learned from our sites is that a sustainable community takes socio-cultural heritage into consideration in its development and provides opportunities for the ongoing production and reproduction of cultural experiences and expressions. Culture is enacted through language, ritual, symbolism and storytelling. Another way to think about culture is as a kind of remembering. Through culture, stories are passed down from one generation to the next, and we remember who we are and where we come from. Culture can also be created anew and provide the opportunity for forging new identities and belongings. Cultural identity can be a powerful motivator for actions, and it becomes easier for people to adhere to sustainability if it is built into a set of cultural values. At the cohousing communities of EVC and TVC and the intentional communities of LA Ecovillage and Twin Oaks, the official statements of values serve as a cultural artifact, publicly announcing the cultural ideals of the community. As these statements included environmental sustainability, part of this cultural statement is a commitment to being better environmental stewards. The act of becoming a community member at LAEV and Twin Oaks, for example, means officially agreeing to adhere to these values. In this way, culture binds people to one another as well as to the larger goal of sustainability.

We also remember, through culture, our relationship to the environment. Culture is an important source of knowledge about taking care of the land.[1] In Oujé-Bougoumou the literal taking of land resulted in loss of community: people were scattered and the ability to transmit and share cultural knowledge was disrupted. More recent reclaiming of the land has helped to reverse that loss. By being together in one place again and because that place has maintained and preserved the wilderness, the Oujé-Bougoumou people are once again able to resume and share cultural practices, including a commitment to and knowledge of their homeland. Culture and indigenous knowledge can be lost, but these can also be re/generated.

Whether it is sustaining a traditional culture or creating the possibility for the emergence of a new one, a project, to be successful, must address socio-cultural heritages and visions. Respecting the cultural roots of a place can be seen at Dockside where it meant integrating input and participation from First Nations communities whose native land the project occupies. At Chez Soi, the socio-cultural heritage of the buildings and community spaces was central to the new Benny Farm project. While Chez Soi is an alternative and innovative building, it was developed with attention to the socio-culture of prior tenants and earlier community. So it is at LAEV which inhabited a building with pre-existing tenants. The founders of the ecovillage were committed to not displacing anyone and, further, to maintaining affordability for those people should they choose to stay. LAEV also provides an example of renovation over new construction, a best practice for meeting the scale and form of other buildings in the community and one which fully embraces socio-cultural context.

Culture

- Who are the previous and potential tenants? What are the cultural legacies of those who lived there before and those targeted as future tenants?
- What kinds of cultural values and ideals might be shared amongst members of the emergent community?
- What kinds of knowledge and practices might be promoted? And what are some best ways to do so?
- What are the cultural mechanisms that support the reproduction of these ideals, values, knowledge and practices?

2 – Context

The second lesson learned is that a sustainable community addresses context. As sociologists, we think of context as location in time and place. While seemingly abstract, context is also deeply concrete. It includes broad social, political and economic forces, but it also includes the material placement of roads, services, trees and towns.

Importantly, context cannot be built; it is already present and shapes people's lives. It is part of the history of a place and is woven into the ordinary routines of the people who live there. Economic and political forces shape how and if developments get off the ground in the first place. At Folsom/Dore, for example, the history of the SOMA neighborhood as a center of social activism shaped the fabric of this affordable, supportive housing program. The developers knew this history and incorporated it by bringing multiple citizen stakeholders to the table in their planning process.

While context can't be built, it can and must be taken into consideration in planning and design. For developers, for example, when questions of context are asked the result is better decisions about where to locate a building so that it is far from sensitive habitats and close to commercial amenities, services and transportation. It may also effect how a building is oriented to take advantage of sun, shade, rain or other elements. New Urbanism, LEED-ND, the principles upon which cohousing and ecovillages are built — all of these mandate taking context into consideration in choosing one's site. We saw it at Takoma and Eastern Village which were explicitly sited near transportation systems, independent businesses, farmers markets, art centers and in a region with a history of progressive actions. As a result of this context, the daily walk to the bus or train station, the ability to get groceries, to go to the post office, to take your child to the local playground, or to engage in a civic or political activity all help make these communities sustainable.

While most of the communities we visited emphasized walkability and proximity to services or transportation, we saw at Cazadero that other kinds of contexts can promote living green as well. There, the context was the natural environment unencumbered by many of the trappings of modern life. As with Thoreau's cabin, such a location provides access to a deep connection with the planet that is crucial to sustainability projects overall.

The lesson of context teaches that designers of green communities first and foremost need to start with place. Understanding the fabric and contours of where they are is necessary to achieve their goals.

Context

- What does the site (i.e., the neighborhood and geographical features) offer?
- What are the local political and policy contexts? Developers, green and traditional, know very well the importance of understanding these contexts for prospective projects.
- Does the project protect or improve existing contextual conditions such as number of trees and access of roads?
- Does architectural quality meet the fabric of neighborhood without shying away from innovations in space, form, light and technologies?

3 – Citizenship

The World Health Organization includes citizenship as one of their prerequisites for health, political will and public support. At the heart of the process of health promotion, they argue, is "the empowerment of communities, their ownership and control of their own endeavours and destinies."[2] Basically, people need to feel included in decisions that affect them. They need to feel like their voices are heard, are important and have the ability to affect outcomes in order to be healthy and happy. Some researchers refer to this as "a sense of mattering."[3] Here, we talk about it as citizenship.[4] While citizenship includes the legal rights and benefits afforded to people by states and governments, it also includes the rights both to have basic needs met — like shelter (including the right to safe housing) and dignity — and to participate in political, social and economic processes through citizen organizations, activist groups or as individuals bringing their voices to the group.

Citizenship, for us, is more than an abstract concept. It includes the very pragmatic and concrete actions associated with struggles for equity. One of the things we learned in our interviews was that much of the work of building sustainable communities involves the tedium of dealing with bureaucracies, endless negotiations with policies and zoning laws and the ability to engage with various levels of local, state, provincial and national governments. In many jurisdictions across North America, for example, ordinances prohibit hanging laundry out to dry or building residential properties next to commercial ones. Building sustainable communities may require challenging such ordinances and, thus, demands engaged citizens who not only feel like they have a voice, but are not afraid to use it. It requires learning the language of politics and policies and feeling entitled to participate in the democratic process.

At the sustainable communities we visited, we saw explicit efforts to empower and engage the multiple voices of those who have stakes in the communities. Within cohousing and ecovillage models, all members have equal opportunity for participation, leadership roles and access to information. In addition, there are systems in place to increase and sustain communication and input. At Twin Oaks note cards and clipboards offer public forums for discussion. The notes equalize the playing field in the sense that even those who may feel disempowered to speak in public forums have a place to assert their opinions. At cohousing and ecovillages there are regular meetings with consensus models to ensure everyone has a voice and that there is a forum to express it. An extremely important way cohousers ensure this kind of citizenship is by being involved in the design and construction of their communities. They themselves are developers.

In another way, citizenship is maximized at many of the sustainable communities we visited by the very fact of providing affordable green housing to people who would otherwise not have access. The social housing/green housing models of Benny Farm and Folsom/Dore in and of themselves promote citizenship by enacting housing as a right and providing dignified shelter for many whose disability, age, or income might otherwise exclude them. At Oujé-Bougoumou, providing people with housing was a conscious, political strategy meant to empower people who had been disenfranchised because they lacked access to home ownership in the past.

Chez Soi, Oujé-Bougoumou, LAEV and Folsom/Dore all provide for sustainable, long-term affordability. This is also the case for the below-market sector of Dockside: a permanent covenant is in place to ensure that affordable units stay affordable. How they provide affordable housing is as important as the fact that they do. At the multi-income Folsom/Dore apartments, for example, affordable units are not distinct from market rent units. As a result, while the residents in what was previously termed

Citizenship

- Are there opportunities for people to voice their opinions and concerns and to engage in action?

- Do community members feel that they have a stake in the community?

- What kinds of organizational structures are in place to provide access to fair and decent housing?

- Can people afford to live here and remain living here as expenses rise and incomes ebb and flow?

- Does the community minimize social stigma and enhance social capital?

- How is the community set up to engage with local municipalities to remove obstacles to living green? What ordinances exist or can be suggested to this end?

housing projects often suffered from social stigma associated with segregated housing and alienation from other neighborhoods, the formerly homeless residents at Folsom/Dore are integrated with people with higher incomes and in multi-ethnic and income-diverse neighborhoods.

4 – Commitment

Green buildings and communities are possible because of the creative and committed energies of residents as well as designers, developers, architects, engineers, builders and others. A fourth lesson is to harness, sustain and enhance this commitment. As we've heard time and again, it's not the buildings that make a community green — it's the people. People compost, recycle, cut down on personal energy use, drive less or not at all, buy local produce or grow their own, participate in local economies, teach their children about all of these things, share resources and consume less.[5] We've argued throughout this book that there are ways to build communities that will make it easier for people to live green, but achieving the commitment of them to do so is critical for success.

Perhaps the most important thing for the ongoing maintenance of sustainable community is the buy-in and commitment of the people who live there. Commitment is often an outcome of successful citizenship: when people are given a voice and involved they are more likely to commit to the task at hand. It seems quite simple, but without this commitment and cooperation, a community cannot be green. It is common for a first wave of residents to be committed, but more difficult to maintain those ideals and energy over time or to organically enlist newcomers to live with the same degree of dedication. There need to be mechanisms in place to support early advocates and to foster newcomer energies. Greg Searle, the Executive Director of BioRegional North America, described this issue in the "Lessons Learned from BedZED" report, put together with Rodney Wilts. Noting the importance of maintaining commitment over the long haul, they advised, "It is helpful to harness the great energy found when residents first move in, and find ways that individuals or organizations adopt events to ensure they continue."[6] From fun events, gatherings and contests to meetings, committees and delegation, keeping people involved is key to success.

At the sites we visited, one way communities achieved and maintained buy-in was through specific workshops designed to inform people about green features or help them live more green in some way. The sustainability workshop at Chez Soi is one example; Twin Oaks and LAEV have given or hosted numerous workshops on topics such as permaculture and sustainable community itself. While these inform, they also transmit something less tangible — they generate excitement, stir passion, create motivation. Similarly, commitment is cultivated through weekly or monthly meetings that occur at places like LAEV and the cohousing communities we visited. These are forums in which people can offer their own ideas and energy to the community, and hear those of others. As well, founding principles can serve as official oaths of commitment in places where they exist (ecovillages, cohousing). In a more formal way, the rules at Folsom/ Dore provide a public commitment to living within the bounds of sustainable community. Sometimes technology can enhance commitment: at Dockside Green, we found that the presence of individualized meters that measured energy use in each unit inspired greater commitment to conservation.

Commitment also applies to those who develop sustainable projects. One thing we learned is that it is not always easy to design something as different as a sustainable community. As we describe above, resistance from multiple angles — zoning laws that are unbending, lack of financial

Commitment

- Who are the essential people from whom commitment must be secured? How can they be supported to maintain that commitment over time?

- To whom will the baton be passed? How will you recognize whose commitment will be required at the next phase?

- How can the early energy and enthusiasm of the developers and builders be harnessed for the future when difficulties may arise?

- How can the early energy and enthusiasm of residents be harnessed for the future ongoing maintenance of the community?

- What mechanisms — events, places, people — are in place to maintain commitment over time?

backing, an unwillingness to do things differently and many others —
commonly arise. Thus, it takes a passionately devoted group of people to
get things done. Burnout is a risk here, and it's important to think about
and strategize for ways of maintaining that commitment on the part of
designers and developers. Daniel Pearl, who faced a particularly long
struggle in the development of Chez Soi, described how he and his partner Mark Poddubiuk traded off in the tough years: one would work
exclusively on Benny Farm while the other attended to the rest of the
work in the office, and then they'd switch. This kept them from burning
out (as well as keeping their office afloat).

5 – Collaboration

The fifth lesson is collaboration: multi-disciplinarity and the involvement of diverse viewpoints and voices are crucial to the development and
ongoing maintenance of a sustainable community. This is well known
within the green building movement and certainly at many of the sites
we visited, where design charettes regularly include participation from
many different perspectives, disciplines and constituencies: engineers,
architects, landscape architects, owners, users, urban planners, developers, social scientists, community organizers and others. An integrative
design process (IDP), for example, is used to create a multi-layered project that can be truly sustainable. LEED itself is an amalgamation of best
practices from multiple disciplines. No one view can capture the holistic
reality of a green community, and successful projects see multi-disciplinarity and collaboration as assets.

Simultaneously, collaboration can occur at different tiers: micro/local,
meso/ state and municipal, macro/federal, as well as be organized top
down or bottom up. Many green developments of the future will continue to require collaboration and broad-based coalitions among multiple
branches of government, financing agencies and industry professionals as
well as local merchants and neighbors. We saw this at Dockside, Chez
Soi and Folsom/Dore where multiple agencies came together to finance,
design and actually build these developments.

The concept of permaculture provides a fitting metaphor for this lesson. Disparate elements work together to create a more balanced, diverse

and productive whole. Understanding that things are interconnected, and thus paying attention to the ways one thing impacts another, and pulling from the strength found in difference are necessary to build a strong sustainable community. The metaphor of permaculture reminds us that collaboration is not all consensus and harmony, but that stinging bugs, parasites, hungry creatures and blights have their place too. Bringing opposing views and groups to the table must be allowed for successful projects to take place. The consensus model provides an opportunity to see the benefits of collaboration in action. At LAEV, for instance, weekly meetings operate on consensus. Many strong personalities and people with different approaches to collaboration often occupy the room, and consensus is not always an easy path. People voice opposing views, get angry and annoyed. But each is committed to listening, so multiple perspectives are heard — and while it's not always possible to reach consensus at every meeting (and consequently decisions get postponed), once it does happen, it is the result of a very thorough process. Other methods of decision-making like dynamic governance also provide fitting examples of collaboration in action.

Collaboration

- Who are the various stakeholders that will converge in developing the project?
- Which perspectives might be most relevant to this project? At which time?
- What mechanisms are in place for listening to those perspectives?
- How can collaboration be encouraged on an ongoing basis?

6 – Connectedness

Community connectedness and social capital are consistently strong indicators of better health status and improved life satisfaction in a wide range of research across diverse settings. Making connection with people is central to living green. Connecting is an activity of reciprocity and collaboration. As the Canadian Cohousing Network describes it, "A deep sense of connectedness to others can lead to radical realignment of personal priorities

… Such values can broaden into concern for the welfare of those unknown and those yet unborn — which is the essence of sustainability."[7] While there is some degree of magic and spontaneity about why and how people connect with one another, we found that successful sustainable communities build in events and spaces that inspire connections to occur.[8] We saw the importance of a *third place* in the dining room at Chez Soi, the community kitchens and living rooms at LAEV, TVC, EVC, the kitchen at Twin Oaks and the rooftop garden at Dockside. At Twin Oaks, LAEV, EVC and TVC there are regular events: meals, parties and holiday celebrations that give people the opportunity, should they want it, to be with others. At Chez Soi, weekly game nights offered predictable possibilities for connecting. Ongoing meetings can also provide opportunities for interactions. Aspects of the built environment also play a key role in maximizing connectedness: mechanisms such as exterior stairwells increase social interaction of residents with each other and increase the ability of adults to supervise children; a green roof increases opportunities for all people to spend time together.

It is also important for a sustainable community to maintain its connections with the larger milieu of which it is a part. We saw at LAEV, for example, an explicit effort to include neighbors in events to expand the scope of their community. Communities that resist insularity work better than those that don't: people within the community have access to a greater number of things, and positive changes occurring inside are able to spread out and influence the neighborhood and larger society. The goal

Connectedness

- Does the built environment offer public and semi-public spaces in which people can gather or commune?
- Does the community provide people with companionship?
- Does it enhance connection with others through organized activities and opportunities for gathering within the community?
- Does the community forge connection with its neighborhood as well as the larger town/city/area?

should not be to create an enclave or gated community, but to foster flow into and out of community.

7 – Care

An ethic of care was in ample evidence at all of the sites we visited and is a significant ingredient in the formula for successful sustainable living. An ethic of care means that people are able to think beyond their own needs. This can include helping others or aiding in the seemingly abstract ideals of social and environmental justice. This is evident in many of the examples we have already mentioned associated with citizenship, commitment and connectedness: communities which cultivate an ethic of care are communities where people are more likely to take positive actions toward making the world around them a better place to live.

Here, we want to talk specifically about the way an ethic of care can encourage people to take care of each other and how communities can build in mechanisms to ensure people are well cared for. Caregiving was a value written into the founding principles for many of the sites. At Takoma Village Community, for instance, there is an official care team which provides an organized mechanism for recognizing community members' needs (i.e., a death in someone's family, a new baby, an illness) and meeting those needs (i.e., food baskets, a listening ear, a ride to an appointment, a professional consultation). This formal committee supplements an informal network of neighbors caring for neighbors — an ethernet site for the community provides a means for people to ask for help, find out if someone is going to the store and could pick up some milk or ask for an emergency babysitter. What was evident in our interviews with cohousers was that this network of formal and informal care creates an environment of social sustainability. People are able to live more comfortably for longer because they know they are well taken care of and, more importantly, they know the specific mechanisms through which they can access that care.

While the ways people care for each other in sustainable communities is important both for the receiving and the giving, it's also true that it's not enough to depend on informal care. Access to formal care and services must be enhanced in order for a community to be truly sustainable.

At Folsom/Dore such care was available on-site, and at Chez Soi and others, it was available in close proximity. By asserting this kind of care, sustainable communities proactively promote health and well-being as well as mitigate the effects of ill health when they do occur. Indeed, the majority of us will get old and want to age in community, and many of us will spend some years of our lives living with chronic illness and disabilities. In order to be sustainable, communities should consider that health is not living disease free; it is an ability to maximize one's well-being. Difficulties will inevitably arise, and sustainable communities build in care services, networks to access care and assurance that needed services are in close proximity. It also means creating built environments that minimize barriers to mobility and accommodate people's changing physical needs throughout the lifecourse.

In a broader sense, a sustainable community cares for the health and well-being of its members by being a place which actively promotes well-being. Dockside Green, for instance, provided inviting, convenient, all-season access to active lifestyles and healthful diets. All of the sites protected the good health of residents by reducing health and safety risks in the built environment: minimizing pollutants, toxins and dangerous chemicals, maximizing pedestrian safety and so on.

Care

- What kinds of possibilities are there for people to express needs and for other people to lend a hand?
- How does the community care for people of different incomes, abilities and ages?
- Does the community promote health and well-being?
- Does it prevent ill health and injury by reducing risks to health in the built environment?
- Does it provide supports when people are in physical or emotional need?
- Does it provide access to resources?

8 – Contact

The eighth lesson for a sustainable community is contact with nature. Much has been written in recent years about the relationship between nature, human health and well-being. Even passive contact with nature (a view from a window) is shown to have beneficial effects on people's health, and the dearth of interaction with natural and wild spaces amongst children is linked to a variety of problems — a phenomenon Richard Louv terms *nature-deficit disorder*.[9] We found that at each community site, people were engaged in concrete actions — tactile, sensory and interactive — that increased their connections with the natural world. These provided a means of feeling connected to the Earth and nature. One of the things that makes all of the communities we visited work so well is the access to shared green spaces, gardens and, for some, open wilderness. Even in urban communities, gardens, windows and patios proliferated. At LAEV, not only the grounds of the buildings themselves were planted, but the adjoining streets were planted with fruit trees, an activity in which the whole neighborhood was involved and which gave local kids a sense of the value and pleasure of nature. Those communities already located in wilder places — Cazadero, Oujé-Bougoumou — maintain the contours of the natural landscape while facilitating connection.

The way nature can nourish human health and well-being highlights the reciprocity of the relationship between humans and nature: just as nature cares for us, when we encourage contact we are more likely to want to care for nature. Margaret Fabrizio's love affair with the land at Cazadero captures the way deep feelings for a particular landscape can instill a lifelong commitment to maintain and care for a particular piece of the planet.

Contact

- Are there shared green spaces and/or gardens built into the communities?
- Are there easy and convenient ways for people to access public green space?
- Are there views of natural environments from residences?
- Is the natural world woven into the built environment?

9 – Commons

The ninth lesson is that of commons: the value of sharing. Vandana Shiva talks about the importance of viewing the planet as a commons rather than as a patchwork of private property.[10] Rather than a model of enclosures, the model of the commons understands the Earth and its resources as shared gifts. Perhaps the most practical and specific lesson we learned about what makes a community sustainable over time is the way that sharing resources enables people to live higher quality lives with less of an environmental impact and therefore for a longer duration of time before resources are depleted.

We've already talked about the idea of common spaces and the way these enhance connections among people, can inspire commitment and facilitate care and citizenship. We add to that the importance of common resources. Regardless of whether the development is a mainstream condo or a commune, commitment to the idea of shared resources is important. At virtually every site we visited there was some kind of car share program, formal or informal. It enabled the community as a whole to have less car ownership and each individual person to spend less time in the car. At communities where there were significant shared spaces — LAEV, TVC, EVC, Twin Oaks — each individual was able to live happily with less square footage. Shared guest rooms, for instance, meant each person didn't need one. The result is less space to heat, to cool — less of a footprint overall. Tool shares, toy shares, clothes swaps were all common and keep consumption down. At Dockside Green, Chez Soi and Oujé-Bougoumou, we also saw shared green infrastructures.

Commons

- Are there any opportunities for shared spaces or infrastructures instead of individual ones?
- What resources can be made available as a shared good?
- What kinds of spaces, technologies or events could help people practice the ongoing sharing of resources?

10 – Continuity

Finally, the tenth lesson that with the others contributes to a sustainable community is the ability to maintain the community over time. Twin Oaks provides a good example of successful maintenance as it is widely regarded as one of North America's more successful communes; it has endured for a long time and lived through much change and upheaval. Flexibility was one of the things that we found has helped it to survive so long. While Twin Oaks held to some central principles, it was flexible and willing to change over time. Kat Kincaid, the original founder, moved away from Twin Oaks feeling that the original ideals and culture of the community had shifted toward countercultural lifestyles and away from the political ideals she and other founders had envisioned. Toward the end of her life, however, she returned, recognizing a different historical context and a need for both to coexist.

Making sure a community is sustainable over time requires the nine lessons posited above, but it also requires constant reflection, accountability, measurement and willingness to change over time. In our interview with Daniel Simons, an architect with David Baker + Partners, he spoke of the need to conduct post-occupancy evaluations (POE), energy use assessments and other process research. He wanted to know not only how the building was performing but what aspects were working best with the humans inside. This was his way of being accountable to the goals he and others set prior to building the apartments. For a community to truly be sustainable over time, ongoing evaluation plans need to be built in, as well as financing to ensure these take place. A sustainable community will make changes necessary in light of scientific evaluation to work toward more economical, environmental and socially sustainable technologies, systems and practices. These changes can include improving upon what is already there as well as adding innovations as they arise.

Continuity

- How does the community perform today and how will this be measured over time?
- Is the community achieving the social and community goals it set out to do in its original mission?
- Is it adhering to ethical standards and practices?
- Is there ongoing participation of stakeholders?
- Is it maintaining the facilities and addressing needs as they arise?
- What is the long-term impact on the community fabric?

We started this book with the intent to better understand the complex ways that social issues are already deeply embedded within built environments. Buildings have material effects on the people who reside inside them, and in turn, people can enhance or serve as barriers to the efficiency, meanings and operation of buildings. As we conclude this book, we leave our readers with ten Cs of social sustainability with the hope — and intent — that they can be used to guide future developments, renovations and community initiatives. Each C is highly connected with the others; together they highlight how much can be accomplished and has already been accomplished to develop true sustainability. Very simple innovations can have big impacts — impacts which are felt across the ten Cs of social sustainability. A community garden, for instance, enhances contact with nature, can provide a gathering place to increase connections with each other, can enhance health and well-being by being a resource for healthful eating and can provide an economic benefit. Using local materials means that local economies are strengthened, and communities, families and individual lives are enhanced. Installing a geothermal system, a green roof or another innovative technology lowers heating bills and increases affordability, improving residents' capacity to age in place. What we did not include here is an eleventh C: Community. It is our belief that community is at the heart of social sustainability and that truly living with a community spirit is the simplest path to living green.

Endnotes

Living Green — an Introduction

1. We are using the term North America to refer to the US and Canada. Mexico was not included in our analysis, and many of the claims made here about "North America", would not be true for Mexico. We recognize that this is an imperfect solution.

2. We have found it to be a taken-for-granted assumption that this paradox is an enduring truth, which is one reason why we have been so pleased to see all of the exceptions to it.
   For a thorough explanation of the paradox see Youngentob and Hostetler.

3. See Gieryn for an excellent articulation of a sociological and scientific approach to built environments.

4. Pollan, p. 7.

5. See his *Crabgrass Frontier*, considered by many to be the quintessential history of the American suburbs.

6. Jackson, p. 50.

7. Jackson, p. 3.

8. Agyeman.

9. See Edwards.

10. See Abbaszadeh et al. and Redd.

11. For a detailed, first-hand accounting of this history, see Gottfried.

12. Yudelson, p. 3.

13. See the Build It Green website.

14. See the Congress for the New Urbanism website.

15. See the One Planet Living website.

16. Farr.

17. Jacobs.

18. Putnam, pp. 83-84.

19. McKibben, p. 105.

20. Nic Paget-Clarke.

21. The use of the term *sustainable* to refer to a particular way of living in the world is widely attributed to a 1987 report by the UN's World Commission on the Environment and Development (WCED). In that report, sustainable development was defined as "meeting the needs of the present without compromising the ability of future generations to meet their own needs" — a definition that has firmly embedded itself into popular parlance. The report is often referred to as the Brundtland Report after the chair of the commission Gro Harlem Brundtland, a lifelong activist who was Norway's youngest and first female prime minister. In collaboration with the other members of the commission, she explicitly linked economic and social issues with environmental concerns. Indeed, that was their mandate: the WCED was established in 1984 partially in response to realizing the severity of the Third World debt crisis and then examined the relationship between the environment and global economic development.

22. Hawken, pp. 186-187.

23. The term Triple Bottom Line dates back to the mid 1990's, when management think tank AccountAbility and John Elkington coined the term and developed three factors of corporate responsibility: economic, environmental and social. The term found public currency in Elkington's 1997 book *Cannibals With Forks*.

24. We chose our sites based on certain criteria. First, we aimed to include a diversity of types of sites: we wanted to describe the ways people were living green at a variety of kinds of communities (e.g. communes, cohousing, ecovillages, social housing, condominiums). Further, we wanted to showcase sites with innovative, high-tech

green designs and technologies as well as sites which were sustainable through low-tech practices. Next, we looked for sites that were in rural locations as well as sites which were in urban locations. All of these factors were considered in order to maximize the range of experiences of living green.

25. Our data was derived from interviews with people living at these sites as well as with architects, engineers, developers, property managers and others involved in some aspect of the sites. We also reviewed secondary sources, websites, historical documents, news articles and other written materials and included these in our analysis.

Chapter 1: Back to the Land

1. For example, as people were coming out in large numbers and entering social movements for sexual rights, some were dismayed to find discriminatory attitudes and practices came not only from mainstream culture, but also from the gay and women's liberation movements taking shape. In response, some lesbian feminists advocated autonomous spaces defined by separation from men. For an even smaller number, such separation was practiced by forming land communities that embraced and privileged lesbian identities as either a temporary political strategy or as a lifelong practice. Here the term community was used strategically around both identity and politics. In Southern Oregon, for example, several land-communities developed a lesbian feminist ecopolitics which included opening access to land and transforming relations of rural ownership understood as part of patriarchal-capitalist production. By the mid-1980s, many lesbian separatist communities began to fracture around issues of race, class and gender expression: see Barbara Smith and Beverly Smith. Lesbian poet Jewell Gomez similarly viewed separatist strategies as an erasure of the important connection between men and women of color fighting for civil rights and gay rights. Whether they exist in spite of or in response to these important critiques, many land communities continue and new ones have formed that espouse their own form of feminist ecopolitics: see Joyce Cheney, Marilyn Frye, Charlotte Bunch/The Furies Collective, Charlotte Bunch and Bette Tallen.

2. French feminist Françoise D'Eaubonne coined the term ecofeminism in 1974: see D'Eaubonne. As a movement, ecofeminism took hold in the early 1970s in response to an environmental movement that lacked a feminist analysis and feminist and leftist movements with little concern for nature, animals or ecology. Ecofeminism includes a variety of beliefs and practices from spirituality to animal rights to commitments to challenging various isms — racism, classism, imperialism, heterosexism, ageism — brought forward by the dualisms of Western thinking: see Maria Mies and Vandana Shiva.

3. Twin Oaks Intentional Community. "A Feminist culture ..."

4. Twin Oaks Intentional Community. *Homepage* and *FAQ*.

5. Kat Kinkade 1995, p. 42.

6. Douglas Cardinal has been credited with creating an Indigenous Canadian style of architecture with his curvilinear, organic buildings.

7. Oujé-Bougoumou. "Our Innovation In Designing The New Village — Alternative Energy Program."

8. Oujé-Bougoumou. "Our Vision in Planning the New Village — Major Objectives."

9. Paul Hawken, p. 101.

Chapter 2: Living Green through Cohousing

1. Allowing people to age in place or, more importantly, age in community is one of the notable benefits of cohousing and has spurred an entire movement toward elder cohousing. We discuss this more in Chapter 4.

2. Meltzer's *Sustainable Community* is an excellent study of cohousing, including the various ways it contributes to environmental sustainability.

Chapter 3: An Alternative for Los Angeles

1. Liz Walker.

2. Julian Agyeman, p. 1.

3. Lois Arkin.

Chapter 4: Greening Grey

1. Randall L. Wray.

2. The Chicago heat wave, like subsequent natural disasters linked to global warming (i.e., the heat wave in Europe a few years after Chicago, Hurricane Katrina), acted as a catalyst for Mayor Daly and the Chicago municipality to implement a strong program of greening city buildings.

3. Communities for a Lifetime website.

Chapter 5: Affordable Green Housing

1. "The homeless count in January 2003 found 6,248 homeless people on a one night count. This is a minimum number and does not include people doubled up with friends or relatives or other invisible populations. Approximately 25% of homeless people are working." Coalition on Homelessness, San Francisco.

2. Mayor's Office of Communications.

3. For these histories see Gayle S. Rubin, 1997 and 1998.

4. For a history of this neighborhood, see Kathleen Connell and Paul Gabriel.

5. Jacobs, p. 4.

6. In many ways, this kind of merging of safety and style is a return to earlier architectural forms where security bars were an opportunity to design elaborate cast-iron design features.

Chapter 6: A Love Affair — the Cazadero Nature and Art Conservancy

1. For more on Margaret's life and work, see her website margaretfabrizio.com.

2. We use the term *land art* in its broadest sense to describe a set of mostly American and British artists who create environmental art, landscape art, earth art and other forms of expression that do not harm and refashion the natural landscape or who alter it to make an environmental point.

3. Goldsworthy is the subject of a 2001 documentary feature film "Rivers and Tides."

Chapter 7: Mainstream Green

1. Dolores Hayden, p. 134.

2. For histories of racial segregation and suburban development see Robert Fogelson and David L. Kirp et al.

3. Paul L. Knox.

4. Newland Communities website.

5. Other rating systems and standards are also being followed for new home construction. The National Homebuilder's Association created Model Green Home Building Guidelines which rate homes according to things like resource, energy and water efficiency, lot design and development, homeowner education and global impact. On local levels, other homebuilder's associations have followed suit.

6. Yudelson, p. 59.

7. California Building Standards Commission website.

8. In 2008 Greensburg, Kansas received international acclaim when it was granted a Sustainable Cities Award by the Sustainable Cities Award Program jointly sponsored by the *Financial Times* and the Urban Land Institute. The award honored nine programs from all over the world that incorporate new ideas and perspectives for best practices in sustainable land use.

9. Andres Duany et al.

10. Dockside Green "Our Vision."

11. Dockside Green. "First Nations Roots."

12. Dockside Green. "Signed MOU on Cooperation and Communication," p. 2.

Lessons Learned: The Ten Cs of Social Sustainability

1. One of the very ways that environmental degradation impacts on the social is through the erosion of culture. Paul Hawken estimates that a language goes extinct every few minutes. As the Amazon is clearcut to meet the demands of industrialized nations, for instance, species (including humans) lose habitat each day. Groups are separated from their traditional lands, from each other and from stories, language and knowledge, the passing down of which creates and maintains culture.

2. See World Health Organization website.

3. McMillan and Chavis.

4. Citizenship highlights the workings of power and knowledge, forcing a recognition that these are linked in ways that must be taken into account. Many of the world's poor, for example, are powerless not because they lack education, but because of lack of a stake over resources. The powerful control and own the vast majority of the world's natural landscapes, including a say into what gets built and where. When individuals and groups are able to organize in ways that claim resources or claim a stake in the natural landscape and building codes, these actions are indicative of equity.

5. Malcolm Gladwell put into circulation an idea that many social organizers know well: the tipping point which propels ideas from few to the many, from entrepreneurs to the majority of people.

6. Searle and Wilts, p. 2.

7. Canadian Cohousing Network website.

8. A *third place* can provide a context within which connection can flourish. Sociologist Ray Oldenburg coined the term *third place* to refer to the importance of having a gathering space — a café, teahouse, pub, park, community center — that is not home and not work. Throughout history, such sites have been staging grounds for social change and revolutions and are often cited as critical to the maintenance of sustainable community. See Erik Assadourian.

9. See Louv and also Wilson for theoretical perspectives on the evolutionary roots of humans' deep need to be in natural spaces.

10. Shiva.

Works Cited

Abbaszadeh, S. et al. "Occupant Satisfaction with Indoor Environmental Quality in Green Buildings." *Proceedings of Healthy Buildings 2006*, Vol. III, pp. 365-370. [online]. [cited October 14, 2008]. repositories.cdlib.org/cedr/cbe/ieq/Abbaszadeh2006_HB/.

Agyeman, Julian. *Sustainable Communities and the Challenge of Environmental Justice*. NYU Press, 2005.

Arkin, Lois. "An Eco-Village Retrofit for Los Angeles: Healing an Inner City Neighborhood" in *Communities Directory: A Guide to Cooperative Living*. Fellowship for Intentional Community, 1995.

Assadourian, Erik. "Engaging Communities for a Sustainable World" in Worldwatch Institute. *State of the World 2008: Innovations for a Sustainable Economy*. Norton, 2008, pp. 151-165.

Brown, Phil and Edwin J. Mikkelsen. *No Safe Place: Toxic Waste, Leukemia, and Community Action*. University of California Press, 1997.

Build it Green. "Introducing GreenPoint Rated: Your Assurance of a Better Place to Live." [online]. [cited November 19, 2008]. builditgreen.org/greenpoint-rated.

Bunch, Charlotte. "Learning from Lesbian Separatism." *Ms. Magazine* (November 1976).

Bunch, Charlotte/The Furies Collective. "Lesbians in Revolt." *The Furies: Lesbian/Feminist Monthly*, Vol#1 (January 1972), pp.8-9.

California Building Standards Commision website. [online]. [cited October 29, 2008]. bsc.ca.gov/default.htm.

Canadian Cohousing Network. "Cohousing and Sustainability — Social Sustainability — Change personal attitudes and practices." [online]. [cited October 16, 2008]. cohousing.ca/sustain.htm.

Cheney, Joyce. *Lesbian Land*. Word Weavers Press, 1976.

Clinton, Hillary Rodham. *It Takes a Village and Other Lessons Children Teach Us*. Simon & Schuster, 1996.

Coalition on Homelessness, San Francisco. *Factsheet on Homelessness*. [online]. [cited June 2, 2008]. cohsf.org/eng/resources/factsheets/hfs.php.

Communities for a Lifetime website: communitiesforalifetime.org/.

Congress for the New Urbanism. [online]. [cited October 31, 2008]. cnu.org.

Connell, Kathleen and Paul Gabriel. "The Power of Broken Hearts: The Origin and Evolution of the Folsom Street Fair." LGBT Historical Society. *Folsom Street Fair 2008: 25 years.* [online]. [cited June 30 2008]. folsomstreetfair.org/history/history6.php.

D'Eaubonne, Françoise. *Le féminisme ou la mort* [Feminism or Death]. Pierre Horay, 1974.

Dockside Green. "First Nations Roots." [online]. [cited October 29, 2008]. docksidegreen.com/bottom/your-community-connections/first-nations-roots.html.

Dockside Green. "Our Vision." [online]. [cited October 29, 2008]. docksidegreen.com/community/overview/overview.html.

Dockside Green. "Signed MOU on Cooperation and Communication." [online]. [cited October 29, 2008]. docksidegreen.com/images/stories/bottom/your-community-connections/Signed MOU on Cooperation and Communication[1].pdf.

Duany, Andres, Elizabeth Plater-Zyberk and Jeff Speck. *Suburban Nation: The Rise of Sprawl and the Decline of the American Dream*. North Point Press, 2000.

Edwards, Andres R. *The Sustainability Revolution: Portrait of a Paradigm Shift*. New Society, 2005.

Elkington, John. *Cannibals with Forks: The Triple Bottom Line of 21st Century Business*. New Society, 1997.

Fabrizio, Margaret. website: margaretfabrizio.com.

Farr, Douglas. *Sustainable Urbanism: Urban Design with Nature.* Wiley, 2007.

Fogelson, Robert. *Bourgeois Nightmares: Suburbia, 1870-1930.* Yale University Press, 2005.

Friedman, Avi. *Room for Thought: Rethinking Home and Community Design.* Penguin, 2005.

Frye, Marilyn. "Some Reflections on Separatism and Power" in Diana Tietjens Meyers, ed. *Feminist Social Thought: A Reader.* Routledge, 1997, pp. 406-414.

Gieryn, Thomas F. "What Buildings Do." *Theory and Society*, Vol. 31#1 (February 2002), pp. 35-74.

Gladwell, Malcolm. *The Tipping Point: How Little Things Can Make a Big Difference.* Little Brown, 2002.

Gomez, Jewell. "Out of the Past," in David Deitcher, ed. *The Question of Equality: Lesbian and Gay Politics in America Since Stonewall.* Scribner, 1995, pp 44-45.

Gore, Al. *An Inconvenient Truth: The Planetary Emergency of Global Warming and What We Can Do About It.* Rodale, 2006.

Gottfried, David. *Greed to Green: The Transformation of an Industry and a Life.* Worldbuild , 2004.

Graae, Bodil. "Children Should Have One Hundred Parents." Article, 1967.

Hawken, Paul. *Blessed Unrest: How the Largest Movement in the World Came Into Being and Why No One Saw It Coming.* Viking Penguin, 2007.

Hayden, Dolores. *Building Suburbia: Green Fields and Urban Growth, 1820-2000.* Pantheon, 2003.

Jackson, Kenneth T. *Crabgrass Frontier: The Suburbanization of the United States.* Oxford, 1987.

Jacobs, Jane. *The Death and Life of Great American Cities.* Random House, 1961. Reprinted by Modern Library, 1983.

Kinkade, Kat. "How to Visit an Intentional Community" in *Communities Directory: a Guide to Cooperative Living.* Fellowship for Intentional Community, 1995, pp. 40-45.

Kirp, David L., John P. Dwyer and Larry A. Rosenthal. *Our Town: Race, Housing and the Soul of Suburbia.* Rutgers University Press, 1996.

Klinenberg, Eric. *Heat Wave: A Social Autopsy of Disaster in Chicago.* University of Chicago Press, 2002.

Knox, Paul L. *Metroburbia,* USA. Rutgers University Press, 2008.

Louv, Richard. *Last Child in the Woods: Saving Our Children from Nature-Deficit Disorder.* Algonquin, 2005).

Maier, William C. et al. "Indoor Risk Factors for Asthma and Wheezing among Seattle School Children" Environmental Health Perspectives, Vol. 105#2 (February 1997),: pp. 208-214.

Mayor's Office of Communications. "Mayor Gavin Newsom Celebrates Grand Opening Of The Folsom Dore Apartments." Press Release, April 20, 2005. [online]. [cited October 2, 2008]. sfgov.org/site/mayor_page.asp?id=31381.

McCamant, Kathryn, Charles R. Durrett and Ellen Hertzman. *Cohousing: A Contemporary Approach to Housing Ourselves.* Ten Speed Press, 2nd ed., 1993.

McKibben, Bill. *Deep Economy: The Wealth of Communities and the Durable Future.* Times Books, 2007.

McMillan, David W. and David M. Chavis. "Sense of community: A definition and theory." *Journal of Community Psychology* Vol.14#1 (January 1986), pp. 6-23.

Meltzer, Graham. *Sustainable Community: Learning from the Cohousing Model.* Trafford, 2005.

Mies, Maria and Vandana Shiva. *EcoFeminism.* Zed Books, 1993.

Newland Communities website. [online]. [cited October 29, 2008]. newlandcommunities.com/#setHome.

One Planet Living. [online]. [cited October 31, 2008]. oneplanetliving.org/index.html.

Oujé-Bougoumou. "Our Innovation In Designing The New Village — Alternative Energy Program." [online]. [cited October 22, 2008]. ouje.ca/content/our-story/innovation.php.

Oujé-Bougoumou. "Our Vision in Planning the New Village — Major Objectives." [online]. [cited October 22, 2008]. ouje.ca/content/our-story/vision.php.

Paget-Clarke, Nic. "Interview with Vandana Shiva: The Role of Patents in the Rise of Globalization." *In Motion Magazine.* August 27, 2003.

[online]. [cited October 31, 2008]. inmotionmagazine.com/global/vshiva4_int.html.

Pollan, Michael. *A Place of My Own: The Education of an Amateur Builder.* Bloomsbury, 1997.

Putnam, Robert D. *Bowling Alone: The Collapse and Revival of American Community.* Simon and Schuster, 2000.

Redd, Stephen. "Asthma in the United States: Burden and Current Theories." *Environmental Health Perspectives,* Vol. 110#6 (June 2002), pp. 557-560.

"Rivers and Tides." Thomas Riedelsheimer, Director, 90 min. Skyline Productions, 2001. riversandtides.co.uk/.

Rubin, Gayle S. "Elegy for the Valley of Kings: AIDS and the Leather Community in San Francisco, 1981-1996" in Martin P. Levine et al, eds. *In Changing Times: Gay Men and Lesbians Encounter HIV/AIDS.* University of Chicago Press, 1997, pp. 101-144.

Rubin, Gayle S. "The Miracle Mile: South of Market and Gay Male Leather, 1962-1997" in James Brook et al, eds. *Reclaiming San Francisco: History, Politics, Culture.* City Lights, 1998, pp. 247-272.

Searle, Greg and Rodney Wilts. "Lessons Learned from BedZed." Unpublished report from BioRegional North America, 2008.

Shiva, Vandana. *Earth Democracy: Justice, Sustainability, and Peace.* South End, 2005.

Skinner, B.F. *Walden Two.* Hackett, 2005 [originally published 1948].

Smith, Barbara and Beverly Smith. "Across the Kitchen Table: A Sister-to-Sister Dialogue" in Cherrie Moraga and Gloria Anzaldua, eds. *This Bridge Called My Back: Writings by Radical Women of Color.* Kitchen Table, Women of Color Press, 1983, pp 121 – 125.

Stang, Alanna and Christopher Hawthorne. *The Green House: New Directions in Sustainable Architecture.* Princeton Architectural Press, 2005.

Tallen, Betty. "Lesbian Separatism: A Historical and Comparative Perspective" in Sarah Lucia-Hoagland and Julia Penelope, eds. *For Lesbians Only: A Separatist Anthology.* Onlywomen Press, 1988, pp. 141-143.

Taylor, D. "The Rise of the Environmental Justice Paradigm: Injustice Framing and the Social Construction of Environmental Discourses." *American Behavioral Scientist,* Vol. 43#4 (January, 2000), pp. 508-580.

Thoreau, Henry David. *Walden Or, Life in the Woods and the Duty of Civil Disobedience.* Harper Perennial, 1973.

Twin Oaks Intentional Community. "A Feminist culture ..." [online]. [cited October 22, 2008]. twinoaks.org/community/women/chicks-sticks.html.

Twin Oaks Intentional Community. *Homepage* and FAQ. [online]. [cited October 24, 2008]. twinoaks.org/index.html and twinoaks.org/FAQ.html.

Walker, Liz. *EcoVillage at Ithaca: Pioneering a Sustainable Culture.* New Society, 2005.

Whitman, Walt. *Leaves of Grass: The First (1855) Edition.* Penguin Classics, 1961.

Wilson, Edward O. *Biophilia.* Harvard University Press, 1984.

Woolf, Virginia. *A Room of One's Own.* Harvest, 2005.

World Commission on Environment and Development. *Our Common Future.* Oxford University Press, 1987.

World Health Organization Regional Office of Europe. "Ottawa Charter for Health Promotion, 1986 — Strengthen community action." [online]. [cited July 1, 2008]. euro.who.int/aboutwho/policy/20010827_2.

Wray, L. Randall. "Social Security in an Aging Society." *Review of Political Economy,* Vol. 18#3 (2006), pp. 391-411.

Youngentob, Kara and Mark Hostetler. "Is a New Urban Development Model Building Greener Communities?" *Environment & Behavior,* Vol. 37# 6 (November 2005), pp. 731-759.

Yudelson, Jerry. *The Green Building Revolution.* Island Press, 2007.

Index

About the Authors

LAURA MAMO AND JENNIFER FOSKET are PhD trained sociologists who have each made a career out of documenting people's experiences and ideas as they concern health and everyday living. Jennifer Fosket is an independent researcher and writer living in Berkeley, California. Laura Mamo is Associate Professor of Sociology at the University of Maryland, College Park. They are co-founders of Social Green, a non profit organization engaged in research, education, and consulting about the social implications of green sustainable buildings, spaces, and environments.

Laura Mamo

Jennifer Fosket

If you have enjoyed *Living Green* you might also enjoy other

BOOKS TO BUILD A NEW SOCIETY

Our books provide positive solutions for people who want to
make a difference. We specialize in:

**Sustainable Living • Green Building • Peak Oil • Renewable Energy
Environment & Economy • Natural Building & Appropriate Technology
Progressive Leadership • Resistance and Community
Educational and Parenting Resources**

New Society Publishers

ENVIRONMENTAL BENEFITS STATEMENT

New Society Publishers has chosen to produce this book on Enviro 100, recycled paper made with **100% post consumer waste**, processed chlorine free, and old growth free.

For every 5,000 books printed, New Society saves the following resources:[1]

26	Trees
2,398	Pounds of Solid Waste
2,638	Gallons of Water
3,441	Kilowatt Hours of Electricity
4,359	Pounds of Greenhouse Gases
19	Pounds of HAPs, VOCs, and AOX Combined
7	Cubic Yards of Landfill Space

[1]Environmental benefits are calculated based on research done by the Environmental Defense Fund and other members of the Paper Task Force who study the environmental impacts of the paper industry.

For a full list of NSP's titles, please call **1-800-567-6772** *or check out our website at:*

www.newsociety.com

NEW SOCIETY PUBLISHERS